Welkom!

Just Enough **Dutch**

D. L. Ellis, D. van der Luit

Pronunciation Dr. J. Baldwin

PASSPORT BOOKS

NTC/Contemporary Publishing Company

The **McGraw·Hill** Companies

Library of Congress Cataloging-in-Publication Data

Ellis, D.L.
    Just enough Dutch / D.L. Ellis, D. van der Luit; pronunciation, J. Baldwin.
    157 p. : ill., 1 map ; 17 cm.
    Includes index.
    ISBN 0-8442-9507-8
    1. Dutch language—Conversation and phrase books—English.

  PF121 .E45   1997
  439.31'83421—dc21   97-048945

The publisher would like to thank the Netherlands and Belgian National Tourist
Offices for their help during the preparation of this book.

15 16 17 18 19 20 21 22 23 24 25 26 VRS/VRS 0 9 8 7 6

ISBN 0-8442-9507-8

McGraw-Hill books are available at special quantity discounts to use as
premiums and sales promotions, or for use in corporate training programs. For
more information, please write to the Director of Special Sales, Professional
Publishing, McGraw-Hill, Two Penn Plaza, New York, NY 10121-2298. Or contact
your local bookstore.

This book is printed on acid-free paper.

Contents

Using the phrase book

- This phrase book is primarily designed to help you get by in the Netherlands, to get what you want or need. However, it could also be used in the Flemish part of Belgium (see map p. 11). It concentrates on the simplest but most effective way you can express these needs in an unfamiliar language.
- The CONTENTS on p. 5 gives you a good idea of which section to consult for the phrase you need.
- The INDEX on p. 155 gives more detailed information about where to look for your phrase.
- When you have found the right page you will be given:
  either – the exact phrase
  or   – help in making up a suitable sentence
  and   – help to get the pronunciation right
- The English sentences in **bold type** will be useful for you in a variety of different situations, so they are worth learning by heart. (See also DO IT YOURSELF, p. 147.)
- Wherever possible you will find help in understanding what Dutch people are saying to *you*, in reply to your questions.
- If you want to practise the basic nuts and bolts of the language further, look at the DO IT YOURSELF section starting on p. 147.
- Note especially these three sections:
  Everyday expressions p. 12
  Shop talk p. 56
  Public notices p. 125
  You are sure to want to refer to them most frequently.
- Once abroad, remember to make good use of the local tourist offices (see p. 26).

US addresses:

Netherlands National Tourist Office
225 North Michigan Avenue, Suite 1854
Chicago, IL 60601
1-888-464-6552

Belgian National Tourist Office
780 Third Avenue
New York, NY 10017
(212) 758-8130..34

A note on the pronunciation system

In traveler's phrase books there is usually a pronunciation section which tries to teach English-speaking tourists how to correctly pronounce the language of the country they are visiting. This is based on the belief that in order to be understood, the speaker must have an accurate, authentic accent—that he must pronounce every last word letter-perfectly.

The authors of this book, on the other hand, wanted to devise a workable and usable pronunciation system. So they had to face the fact it is absolutely impossible for an average speaker of English who has no technical training in phonetics and phonetic transcription systems (which includes 98% of all the users of this book!) to reproduce the sounds of a foreign language with perfect accuracy, just from reading a phonetic transcription, cold—no prior background in the language. We also believe that you don't have to have perfect pronunciation in order to make yourself understood in a foreign country. After all, natives you run into will take into account that you are foreigners, and visitors, and more than likely they will feel gratified by your efforts to communicate and will probably go out of their way to try to understand you. They may even help you, and correct you, in a friendly manner. We have found, also, that visitors to a foreign country are not usually concerned with perfect pronunciation—they just want to get their message across, to communicate!

With this in mind, we have designed a pronunciation system which is of the utmost simplicity to use. This system does not attempt to give an accurate—but also problematical and tedious—representation of the sound system of the language, but instead uses common sound and letter combinations in English which are the closest to the sounds in the foreign language. In this way, the sentences transcribed for pronunciation should be read as naturally as possible, as if they were ordinary English. In no way does the user have to attempt to make the words sound "foreign." So, while to yourselves you will sound as if you are speaking ordinary English—or at least making ordinary English sounds—you will at the same time be making yourselves understood in another language. And, as the saying goes, practice makes perfect, so it is probably a good idea to repeat aloud to yourselves several times the phrases you think you are going to use, before you actually use them. This will give you greater confidence, and will also help in making yourself understood.

In Dutch it is important to stress or emphasize the syllables in italics, just as you would if we were to take as an English example: L*i*ttle Jack H*o*rner s*a*t in the c*o*rner. Here we have ten syllables but only four stresses.

Of course you may enjoy trying to pronounce a foreign language as well as possible and the present system is a good way to start. However, since it uses only the sounds of English, you will very soon need to depart from it as you begin to imitate the sounds you hear the native speaker produce and relate them to the spelling of the other language.

Succes!
souk-cess

Groningen

Enschede

Haarlem
Amsterdam
Leiden
Utrecht   Arnhem
Nijmegen
's-Gravenhage
(The Hague)   West Germany

Rotterdam
Dordrecht   's-Hertogenbosch
Breda   Tilburg
Eindhoven

Heerlen-Kerkrade
Maastricht

Belgium

Everyday expressions

[See also 'Shop talk', p. 56]
- Although you will find the correct greetings listed below, the Dutch commonly use **daag** (dahg) to express all of these.

Hello	**Hallo** hull*o*
Good morning	**Goede morgen** h*oo*-der m*o*r-hen
Good afternoon	**Goede middag** h*oo*-der mid-d*u*k
Good day	**Goede dag** h*oo*-der duk
Good evening	**Goede avond** h*oo*-der *a*h-vent
Good night	**Goede nacht** h*oo*-der nukt
Goodbye	**Tot ziens** tot z*ee*ns
See you later	**Tot straks** tot struks
Yes	**Ja** yah
Please	**Alstublieft** uls-too-bl*ee*ft
Great!	**Geweldig!** her-wel-dik
Thank you	**Dank u** dunk oo
Thank you very much	**Dank u wel** dunk oo wel
That's right	**Precies** prer-s*ee*s
No	**Nee** nay
No, thank you	**Nee, dank u** nay dunk oo
I disagree	**Ik ben het er niet mee eens** ik ben et er n*ee*t may ayns
Excuse me	**Pardon** par-d*o*n

Don't mention it	**Geen dank**
	hain dunk
That's good	**Dat is goed**
	dut is hoot
That's no good	**Dat is niet goed**
	dut is neet hoot
I know	**Ik weet het**
	ik wait et
I don't know	**Ik weet het niet**
	ik wait et neet
It doesn't matter	**Het geeft niet**
	et hayft neet
Where's the toilet please?	**Waar is het toilet, alstublieft?**
	wahr is et twah-let uls-too-bleeft
How much is that ? [*point*]	**Hoeveel is dat?**
	hoo-vale is dut
Is the service included?	**Is het inclusief bediening?**
	is et in-cloo-seef ber-deening
Do you speak English?	**Spreekt u engels?**
	spraykt oo eng-els
I am sorry …	**Het spijt me …**
	et spate mer …
I don't speak Dutch	**Ik spreek geen nederlands**
	ik sprayk hane nay-der-lunts
I only speak a little Dutch	**Ik spreek maar een beetje nederlands**
	ik sprayk mahr en bayt-yer nay-der-lunts
I don't understand	**Ik begrijp het/u niet**
	ik ber-hreyp et/oo neet
Please can you …	**Kunt u dat alstublieft …**
	koont oo dut uls-too-bleeft …
repeat that?	**herhalen?**
	her-hah-len
speak more slowly?	**langzamer zeggen?**
	lung-zah-mer zek-en
write it down?	**opschrijven?**
	op-skrey ven
What is this called in Dutch? [*point*]	**Hoe heet dit in het nederlands?**
	hoo hate dit in et nay-der-lunts

Crossing the border

ESSENTIAL INFORMATION

- Don't waste time just before you leave rehearsing what you are going to say to the border officials – the chances are that you won't have to say anything at all, especially if you travel by air.
  It is more useful to check that you have your documents handy for the journey: passports, tickets, money, travellers' cheques, insurance documents, driving licence and car registration documents.
  Look out for these signs:
DOUANE	(customs)
GRENS	(border)
GRENS POLITIE	(frontier police)
  [For further signs and notices, see p. 125]
- You may be asked routine questions by the customs officials *[see below]*. If you have to give personal details, see 'Meeting people' p. 16. The other important answer to know is 'Nothing': Niets (neets).

ROUTINE QUESTIONS

Passport?	**Paspoort?** p*u*s-port
Insurance?	**Verzekering?** ver-*zay*-ker-ing
Registration document? (logbook)	**Auto papieren?** *ow*to pah-*pee*-ren
Ticket, please	**Uw kaartje, alstublieft** oo kart-*yer* uls-too-bl*ee*ft
Have you anything to declare?	**Heeft u iets aan te geven?** h*ay*ft oo eets ahn ter h*ay*ven
Where are you going?	**Waar gaat u heen?** wahr haht oo hayn
How long are you staying?	**Hoe lang blijft u?** hoo lung bleyft oo
Where have you come from?	**Waar komt u vandaan?** wahr komt oo vun-d*ah*n

You may have to fill in forms which ask for:

surname	**achternaam**
first name	**voornaam**
maiden name	**meisjesnaam**
place of birth	**geboorteplaats**
date of birth	**geboortedatum**
address	**adres**
nationality	**nationaliteit**
profession	**beroep**
passport number	**paspoort nummer**
issued at	**uitgegeven te**
signature	**handtekening**

Meeting people

[See also 'Everyday expressions', p. 12]

Breaking the ice

Hello	**Hallo**
	hull*o*
Good morning	**Goede morgen**
	h*oo*-der m*o*r-he*n*
How are you?	**Hoe gaat het?**
	hoo haht et
I am here ...	**Ik ben hier ...**
	ik ben here ...
on holiday	**met vakantie**
	met vah-*k*u*n*-tse*e*
on business	**voor zaken**
	vor *zah*-ken
Can I offer you ...	**Mag ik u ... aanbieden?**
	muk ik oo ... *ahn*-beeden
a drink?	**iets te drinken**
	eets ter dr*i*nken
a cigarette?	**een sigaret**
	en see-hah-r*et*
a cigar?	**een sigaar**
	en see-har
Are you staying long?	**Blijft u lang?**
	bleyft oo lung

Name

What's your name?	**Hoe heet u?**
	hoo hate oo
My name is ...	**Ik heet ...**
	ik hate ...

Family

Are you married?	**Bent u getrouwd?**
	bent oo het-tro*ut*

I am ...	**Ik ben ...**
	ik ben ...
married	getrouwd
	het-tr*o*ut
single	ongetrouwd
	*o*n-het-trout
This is ...	**Dit is ...**
	dit is ...
my wife	mijn vrouw
	mane vrow
my husband	mijn man
	mane mun
my son	mijn zoon
	mane zohn
my daughter	mijn dochter
	mane d*o*kter
my (boy)friend	mijn vriend
	mane vreent
my (girl)friend	mijn vriendin
	mane vreen-d*i*n
my colleague (male or female)	mijn collega
	mane kol-l*a*y-hah
Do you have any children?	**Heeft u ook kinderen?**
	hayft oo oak k*i*n-der-ren
I have ...	**Ik heb ...**
	ik hep ...
one daughter	een dochter
	*a*yn d*o*kter
one son	een zoon
	*a*yn zohn
two daughters	twee dochters
	tway d*o*kters
three sons	drie zoons
	dree zohns
No, I haven't any children	**Nee, ik heb geen kinderen**
	nay ik hep hayn k*i*n-der-ren

Where you live

Are you . . .	Bent u . . .
	bent oo . . .
Dutch?	nederlander/nederlandse?*
	nay-der-lun-der/nay-der-lunt-ser
Belgian?	belg/belgische?*
	belk/bel-heeser
a Surinamer?	surinamer/surinaamse?*
	soo-ree-nah-mer/soo-ree-nahm-ser
I am . . .	Ik ben . . .
	ik ben . . .
American	amerikaan/amerikaanse*
	ah-may-ree-kahn/ah-may-ree-kahn-ser
English	engelsman/engelse*
[For other nationalities, p. 140]	eng-els-mun/eng-el-ser
I live . . .	Ik woon . . .
	ik woan . . .
in London	in Londen
	in lon-den
in England	in Engeland
	in eng-er-lunt
in the north	in het noorden
	in et norden
in the south	in het zuiden
	in et zo-ee-den
in the west	in het westen
	in et westen
in the east	in het oosten
	in et ohs-ten
in the centre	in het centrum
[For other countries, p. 138]	in et centrem

For the businessman and woman

I'm from . . . (firm's name)	**Ik ben van . . .**
	ik ben vun . . .
I have an appointment with . . .	**Ik heb een afspraak met . . .**
	ik hep en *uf*-sprahk met . . .
May I speak to . . .?	**Mag ik met . . . spreken?**
	muk ik met . . . spr*ay*ken
This is my card	**Hier is mijn kaartje**
	here is mane k*a*rt-yer
I'm sorry, I'm late	**Het spijt me dat ik laat ben**
	et spate mer dut ik l*a*ht ben
Can I fix another appointment?	**Kan ik een andere afspraak maken?**
	kun ik en *u*n-der-er *u*f-sprahk m*a*h-ken
I am staying at the hotel . . .	**Ik logeer in hotel . . .**
	ik loh-sh*ee*r in ho-tel . . .

Asking the way

ESSENTIAL INFORMATION

● Keep a look out for all these place names as you will find them on shops, maps and notices.

WHAT TO SAY

Excuse me, please	**Neem me niet kwalijk ...**
	name mer neet kw*ah*-lek
How do I get ...	**Hoe kom ik naar ...**
	hoo kom ik nar ...
to the airport?	**het vliegveld?**
	et vl*ee*k-velt
to Amsterdam?	**Amsterdam?**
	umster-d*um*
to the beach?	**het strand?**
	et strunt
to the bus station?	**het bus station?**
	et b*us* st*a*ts-see-on
to the Centraal hotel?	**het Centraal Hotel?**
	et cen-tr*ah*l hotel
to the Concertgebouw?	**het Concertgebouw?**
	et con-s*ai*rt-her-ba-*oo*
to the Delta Works?	**de Delta Werken?**
	der delta w*ai*rken
to the Kalverstraat?	**de Kalverstraat?**
	der k*u*lver-str*ah*t
to the market?	**de markt?**
	der markt
to the police station?	**het politiebureau?**
	et poh-*lee*-tsee-boo-r*o*
to the post office?	**het postkantoor?**
	et p*o*sst-kun-tor
to the railway station?	**het spoorwegstation?**
	et sp*o*r-wek-st*a*ts-see-on
to the Rijksmuseum?	**het Rijksmuseum?**
	et r*eyk*s-moo-sayem

to the Rokin?	**het Rokin?**
	et rok-kin
to the sports stadium?	**het stadion?**
	et stah-dee-on
to the tourist information office?	**het VVV kantoor?**
	et vay-vay-vay kun-tor
to Utrecht?	**Utrecht?**
	oo-trekt
Excuse me, please	**Neem me niet kwalijk . . .**
	name mer neet kwah-lek . . .
Is there . . . near by?	**Is hier in de buurt . . .**
	is here in der boort . . .
an art gallery	**een kunst galerij?**
	en koonst hah-ler-rey
a baker's	**een bakker?**
	en bukker
a bank	**een bank?**
	en bunk
a bar	**een bar?**
	en bar
a botanical garden	**een botanische tuin?**
	en bo-tah-nee-ser to-een
a bus stop	**een bushalte?**
	en bus-hulter
a butcher's	**een slager?**
	en slah-her
a café	**een café**
	en cuf-fay
a cake shop	**een banketwinkel?**
	en bunket-winkel
a campsite	**een camping?**
	en camping
a car park	**een parkeerterrein?**
	en par-kair-terreyn
a change bureau	**een wissel kantoor?**
	en wissel kuntor
a chemist's	**een drogist?**
	en dro-hist
a church	**een kerk?**
	en kairk
a cinema	**een bioscoop?**
	een bee-os-cope

Is there . . . near by?	Is hier in de buurt . . .
	is here in der boort . . .
a delicatessen	een delicatessen winkel?
	en day-lee-kah-tes-sen winkel
a dentist's	een tandarts?
	en tunt-arts
a department store	een warenhuis?
	en wah-ren-ho-ees
a disco	een disco
	en dis-ko
a doctor's surgery	een dokter?
	en dok-ter
a dry-cleaner's	een stomerij?
	en stomer-rey
a fishmonger's	een viswinkel?
	en vis-winkel
a garage (for repairs)	een garage?
	en hah-rah-zher
a hairdresser's	een kapper?
	en kupper
a greengrocer's	een groentewinkel?
	en hroonter-winkel
a grocer's	een kruidenierswinkel?
	en kro-ee-der-neers-winkel
a hardware shop	een ijzerwinkel?
	en eyzer-winkel
a Health and Social Security Office	een kantoor Gezondheids en Sociale Zorg Dienst?
	en kun-tor her-zont-heyts en soh-see-ah-ler zork deenst
a hospital	een ziekenhuis?
	en zeeken-ho-ees
a hotel	een hotel?
	en ho-tel
an ice-cream parlour	een ijs-salon?
	en eys-sah-lon
a laundry	een wasserij?
	en wusser-rey
a museum	een museum?
	een moo-sayem
a night club	een nacht club?
	en nukt cloop

a park	een park?
	en park
a petrol station	een benzinepompstation?
	en ben-zee-ner-pomp-stats-see-on
a post box	een brievenbus?
	en breeven-bus
a public toilet	een openbaar toilet?
	en open-bar twah-let
a restaurant	een restaurant?
	en res-to-ran
a (snack) bar	een snelbuffet?
	en snel-booffet
a sports ground	een sportterrein?
	en sport-terreyn
a supermarket	een supermarkt?
	en sooper-markt
a sweet shop	een snoepwinkel?
	en snoop-winkel
a swimming pool	een zwembad?
	en zwem-but
a telephone (booth)	een telefoon cel?
	en telefone cel
a theatre	een theater?
	en tay-ah-ter
a tobacconist's	een sigarenwinkel?
	en see-hahren winkel
a travel agent's	een reisbureau?
	en reys-boo-ro
a youth hostel	een jeugdherberg?
	en yerkt-hair-bairk
a zoo	een dierentuin?
	en dee-ren-to-een

DIRECTIONS

- Asking where a place is, or if a place is near by, is one thing; making sense of the answer is another.
- Here are some of the most important key directions and replies.

Left	**Links**
	links
Right	**Rechts**
	rekts
Straight on	**Rechtdoor**
	rekt-dor
There	**Daar**
	dar
First left/right	**Eerste links/rechts**
	air-ster links/rechts
Second left/right	**Tweede links/rechts**
	twayder links/rekts
At the crossroads	**Bij de kruisweg**
	bey der kro-ees-wek
At the traffic lights	**Bij de verkeerslichten**
	bey der ver-k*air*s-lik-ten
At the roundabout	**Bij de rotonde**
	bey der ro-*ton*-der
At the level crossing	**Bij de overweg**
	bey der *over*-wek
It's near/far	**Het is dichtbij/ver**
	et is dikt-b*ey*/v*air*
One kilometre	**Een kilometer**
	ayn k*ee*-lo-mayter
Two kilometres	**Twee kilometer**
	tway k*ee*-lo-mayter
Five minutes ...	**Vijf minuten ...**
	veyf mee-*noo*ten ...
on foot	**lopend**
	*l*opent
by car	**met de auto**
	met der *ow*to

Take ...	Neem ...
	name ...
the bus	de bus
	der bus
the train	de trein
	der train
the tram	de tram
	der trem

[For public transport, see p. 116]

The tourist information office

ESSENTIAL INFORMATION

- Most towns and even some villages in the Netherlands have a tourist information office.
- Look out for the sign shown top right.
- In major towns you will find that in addition the VVV offices also bear the following sign:

- These offices will supply you with information on any region of the Netherlands in the form of leaflets, fold-outs, brochures, lists and plans.
- You may have to pay for some types of document, but this is not usual.
- All offices are open from 9.00 a.m. to 5.00 p.m. weekdays and from 10.00 a.m. to 12.00 p.m. on Saturdays. During the high season, some offices are open during the evenings and on Sunday afternoons.
- For finding a tourist office, see p. 20

WHAT TO SAY

Please, have you got ...	Heeft u ... alstublieft?
	hayft oo ... uls-too-bleeft
a plan of the town?	een stadsplan
	en stuts-plun
a list of hotels?	een hotel lijst
	en ho-tel leyst
a list of campsites?	een lijst van campings
	en leyst vun campings
a list of restaurants?	een lijst van restaurants
	en leyst vun res-to-rans
a list of coach excursions?	een lijst van bus excursies
	en leyst vun bus ex-cur-sees
a list of events?	een lijst van evenementen
	en leyst vun ay-ver-ner-menten
a leaflet on the town?	een blaadje over de stad
	en blaht-yer over der stut
a leaflet on the region?	een blaadje over de omgeving
	en blaht-yer over der om-hayving

Please, have you got . . .	**Heeft u . . . alstublieft?**
	hayft oo . . . uls-too-bleeft
a railway timetable?	**een spoorwegboekje**
	en spoor-wek-book-yer
a bus timetable?	**een bus dienstregeling**
	en bus deenst-rayker-ling
In English, please	**In het engels, alstublieft**
	in et eng-els uls-too-bleeft
How much do I owe you?	**Hoeveel ben ik u schuldig?**
	hoo-vale ben ik oo skooldik
Can you recommend . . .	**Kunt u . . . aanbevelen?**
	koont oo . . . ahn-ber-vaylen
a cheap hotel?	**een goedkoop hotel**
	en hoot-kope ho-tel
a cheap restaurant?	**een goedkoop restaurant**
	en hoot-kope res-to-ran
Can you make a booking for me?	**Kunt u iets voor me reserveren?**
	koont oo eets vor mer ray-ser-vairen

LIKELY ANSWERS

You need to understand when the answer is 'No'. You should be able to tell by the assistant's facial expression, tone of voice and gesture; but there are some language clues such as:

No	**Nee**
	nay
I'm sorry	**Het spijt me**
	et spate mer
I don't have a list of hotels	**Ik heb geen lijst van hotels**
	ik hep hayn leyst vun ho-tels
I haven't got any left	**Ik heb er geen meer**
	ik hep er hayn mair
It's free	**Het is gratis**
	et is hrah-tis

Accommodation

Hotel

ESSENTIAL INFORMATION

- If you want hotel-type accommodation, all the following words in capital letters are worth looking for on name boards:
  HOTEL
  MOTEL
  PENSION (boarding house)
  JEUGDHERBERG (youth hostel)
- A list of hotels in the town or district can usually be obtained at the local tourist office [see p. 26].
- All hotels are listed, the cheaper ones having no star rating, while the more luxurious and expensive having proportionally more stars.
- The cost is displayed in the room itself, so you can check it when having a look round before agreeing to stay.
- The displayed cost is for the room itself, per night and not per person. Breakfast is extra and therefore optional.
- Service and VAT (BTW) is always included in the cost of the room, so tipping is voluntary.
- Not all hotels provide meals, apart from breakfast. A breakfast will consist of coffee/tea, bread (usually rolls), cold meats, cheese, jam and fruit.
- An identity document is requested when registering at a hotel and will normally be kept overnight.
- Finding a hotel, see p. 20.

WHAT TO SAY

I have a booking	**Ik heb een gereserveerde kamer**
	ik hep en her-ray-ser-v*air*-der kah-mer
Have you any vacancies, please?	**Heeft u nog kamers?**
	hayft oo nok k*ah*-mers
Can I book a room?	**kan ik een kamer reserveren?**
	kun ik en k*ah*-mer ray-ser-v*air*en

It's for ...	Het is voor ... et is vor ...
one person	één persoon ayn per-sohn
two people [For numbers, see p. 129]	twee personen tway pair-sohnen
It's for ...	Het is voor ... et is vor ...
one night	één nacht ayn nukt
two nights	twee nachten tway nukten
one week	één week ayn wake
two weeks	twee weken tway waken
I would like ...	Ik zou graag ... ik zow hrahk ...
a room	een kamer en kah-mer
two rooms	twee kamers tway kahmers
with a single bed	met een één-persoonsbed met en ayn-pair-sohns-bet
with two single beds	met twee één-persoonsbedden met tway ayn-pair-sohns-bed-den
with a double bed	met een tweepersoonsbed met en tway-pair-sohns-bet
with a toilet	met toilet met twah-let
with a bathroom	met badkamer met but-kah-mer
with a shower	met douche met doosh
with a cot	met een wieg met en week
I'd like ...	Ik wil het graag ... hebben ik wil et hrahk ... hebben
full board	vol pension vol pun-see-on
half board	half (demi) pension hulf (day-mee) pun-see-on

Do you serve meals?	**Kunnen we hier eten?**
	koonnen wer here *ay*-ten
At what time is ...	**Hoe laat is ...**
	hoo laht is ...
breakfast?	**het ontbijt?**
	et ont-b*eyt*
lunch?	**de lunch?**
	der lunch
dinner?	**het diner?**
	et *dee*-nay
How much is it?	**hoeveel is het?**
	h*oo*-vale is et
Can I look at the room?	**Kan ik de kamer zien?**
	kun ik der k*ah*-mer zeen
I'd prefer a room ...	**Ik heb liever een kamer ...**
	ik hep l*ee*ver en k*ah*-mer ...
at the front/back	**aan de voorkant/achterkant**
	ahn der vor-kunt/ukter-kunt
OK, I'll take it	**Goed, ik neem het**
	hoot ik name et
No thanks, I won't take it	**Nee dank u, deze niet**
	nay dunk oo d*a*zer neet
The key to number (10) please	**De sleutel voor nummer (tien) alstublieft**
	der slertel vor noommer (teen) uls-too-bleeft
Please, may I have ...	**Heeft u ... alstublieft?**
	hayft oo ... uls-too-bl*ee*ft
a coat hanger?	**een klerenhanger**
	en kl*ai*ren-hung-*er*
a towel?	**een handdoek**
	en h*u*n-dook
a glass?	**een glas**
	en hlus
some soap?	**een stuk zeep**
	en stook zap*e*
an ashtray?	**een asbak**
	en *u*s-buk
another pillow?	**nog een kussen**
	nok en koossen
another blanket?	**nog een deken**
	nok en d*a*yken

*Use the first alternative for men, the second for women.

Come in!	**Kom binnen!**
	kom b*i*nnen
One moment, please!	**Een ogenblik alstublieft!**
	en *o*h-hen-blik uls-too-bl*ee*ft
Please can you ...	**Kunt u ... alstublieft?**
	koont oo ... uls-too-bl*ee*ft
do this laundry/dry-cleaning?	**dit laten wassen/stomen**
	dit l*a*h-ten wussen/st*o*men
call me at ... ?	**me om ... roepen**
	mer om r*oo*-pen
help me with my luggage?	**me met mijn bagage helpen**
	mer met mane bah-h*a*h-sher helpen
call me a taxi for ... ?	**een taxi voor me bestellen**
[For times, see p. 131]	en tuksee vor mer ber-stellen
The bill, please	**De rekening, alstublieft**
	der r*a*yker-ning uls-too-bl*ee*ft
Is service included?	**Is het inclusief bediening?**
	is et in-cloo-seef ber-d*ee*-ning
I think this is wrong	**Ik denk dat dit verkeerd is**
	ik denk dut dit ver-k*ai*rt is
May I have a receipt?	**Mag ik een kwitantie hebben?**
	muk ik en kwee-t*u*n-tsee hebben

At breakfast

Some more ... please	**Nog wat ... alstublieft**
	nok wut ... uls-too-bl*ee*ft
coffee	**koffie**
	k*o*ffee
tea	**thee**
	tay
bread	**brood**
	broht
butter	**boter**
	boh-ter
jam	**jam**
	shem
May I have a boiled egg?	**Mag ik een gekookt ei?**
	muk ik en her-kohkt ey

LIKELY REACTIONS

Have you an identity
   document, please?

Heeft u een identiteitsbewijs,
   alstublieft?
hayft oo en ee-den-tee-*taits*-
   ber-weys uls-too-bleeft

What's your name? [*see p. 16*]

Wat is uw naam?
wut is oo nahm

Sorry, we're full

Het spijt me, we zijn vol
et spate mer wer zane vol

I haven't any rooms left

Ik heb geen kamers meer
ik hep hane *kah*-mers mair

Do you want to have a look?

Wilt u even kijken?
wilt oo *ay*-ven kai-ken

How many people is it for?

Voor hoeveel personen is het?
vor *hoo*-vale pair-*soh*-nen is et

From (seven o'clock) onwards

Vanaf (zeven uur)
vun-*af* (*zay*-ven oor)

From (midday) onwards
[*For times, see p. 131*]

Vanaf (twaalf uur's middags)
vun-*af* (twahlf oor smid-duks)

It's (30) guilders
[*For numbers, see p. 129*]

Het is (dertig) gulden
et is (*dairtik*) hoolden

Camping and youth hostelling

ESSENTIAL INFORMATION
Camping

- Look for the words **CAMPING** or **KAMPEERTERREIN** and this sign.

- Be prepared to have to pay:
  per person
  for the car
  for the tent or caravan plot
  for electricity
  for hot showers
- You must provide proof of identity, such as your passport.
- Officially recognized campsites have a star rating: the more stars, the better equipped.
- Camping is regulated by local and provincial by-laws. Lists are available from the VVV.
- Off-site camping is not permitted.

Youth hostels

- Look for the word: **JEUGDHERBERG**
- You must have a YHA card.
- The charge for the night is the same for all ages, but some hostels are dearer than others.
- You must bring your own sleeping bag lining.
- Accommodation is usually provided in small dormitories.
- Food and cooking facilities vary from place to place and you may also have to help with jobs.
- For buying or replacing camping equipment, see p 54.

WHAT TO SAY

I have a booking	**Ik heb gereserveerd** ik hep her-ray-ser-*vairt*
Have you any vacancies?	**Heeft u nog iets vrij?** hayft oo nok eets vrey
It's for ...	**Het is voor ...** et is vor ...
one adult/person	**één volwassene/persoon** ayn vol-*wusserner*/pair-*sohn*
two adults/people	**twee volwassenen/personen** tway vol-*wusserernen*/pair-soh-nen
and one child	**en één kind** en ayn kint
and two children	**en twee kinderen** en tway kin-der-en
It's for ...	**Het is voor ...** et is vor
one night	**één nacht** ayn nukt
two nights	**twee nachten** tway nukten
one week	**één week** ayn wake
two weeks	**twee weken** tway waken
How much is it ...	**Hoeveel is het ...** *hoo*-vale is et ...
for the tent?	**voor de tent?** vor der tent
for the caravan?	**voor de caravan?** vor der *caravan*
for the car?	**voor de auto?** vor der *owto*
for the electricity?	**voor de elektriciteit?** vor der ay-lek-tree-see-*tait*
per person?	**per persoon?** pair pair-sohn
per day/night?	**per dag/nacht?** pair duk/nukt
May I look round?	**Mag ik even rondkijken?** muk ik *ay*-ven rond-kaiken

Do you close the door/gate at night?	**Sluit u de deur/het hek 's avonds?** slo-eet oo der der/et hek sahvents
Do you provide anything ...	**Serveert u iets ...** sair-vairt oo eets ...
to eat?	**te eten?** ter ay-ten
to drink?	**te drinken?** ter drinken
Do you have ...	**Heeft u ...** hayft oo ...
a bar?	**een bar?** en bar
hot showers?	**warm douches?** warmer dooshes
a kitchen?	**een keuken?** en kerken
a laundry?	**een wasserij?** en wusser-rey
a restaurant?	**een restaurant?** en res-to-ran
a shop?	**een winkel?** en winkel
a swimming pool?	**een zwembad?** en zwem-but

[For food shopping, see p. 62, and for eating and drinking out, see p. 82]

Where are ...	**Waar zijn ...** wahr zane ...
the dustbins?	**de vuilnisbakken?** der vo-eel-nis-bukken
the showers?	**de douches?** der dooshes
the toilets?	**de toilets?** der twah-lets
At what time must one ...	**Hoe laat moet men ...** hoo laht moot men ...
go to bed?	**naar bed?** nar bet
get up?	**opstaan?** op-stahn

Please, have you got . . .	Heeft u alstublieft *hayft oo uls-too-bleeft* . . .
a broom?	een bezem? *en bay-zem*
a corkscrew?	een kurketrekker? *en koorker-trekker*
a drying-up cloth?	een theedoek? *en tay-dook*
a fork?	een vork *en vork*
a fridge?	een koelkast? *en kool-kust*
a frying pan?	een koekepan? *en kooker-pun*
an iron?	een strijkijzer? *en streyk-eyzer*
a knife?	een mes? *en mess*
a plate?	een bord? *en bort*
a saucepan?	een pan? *en pun*
a teaspoon?	een theelepel? *en tay-laypel*
a tin opener?	een blikopener? *en blik-opener*
any washing powder?	wat zeeppoeder? *wut zape-pooder*
any washing-up liquid?	een afwasmiddel? *en ufwus-middel*
The bill, please	De rekening, alstublieft *der rayker-ning uls-too-bleeft*

Problems

The toilet	Het toilet *et twah-let*
The shower	De douche *der doosh*
The tap	De kraan *der krahn*
The razor point	Het scheer-contact *et skair-contuct*

The light	Het licht
	et likt
. . . is not working	. . . werkt niet
	. . . wairkt neet
My camping gas has run out	Ik heb geen kampgas meer
	ik hep hane kump-hus mair

LIKELY REACTIONS

Have you an identity document?	Heeft u een identiteitsbewijs?
	hayft oo en ee-den-tee-taits-ber-weys
Your membership card, please	Uw lidmaatschap-kaart, alstublieft
	oo lit-maht-skup-kart uls-too-bleeft
What's your name? [see p. 16]	Wat is uw naam?
	wut is oo nahm
Sorry, we're full	Het spijt me, we zijn vol
	et spate mer wer zane vol
How many people is it for?	Voor hoeveel personen is het?
	vor hoo-vale pair-soh-nen is et
How many nights is it for?	Voor hoeveel nachten is het?
	vor hoo-vale nukten is et
It's (12) guilders . . .	Het is (twaalf) gulden . . .
	et is (twahlf) hool-den . . .
per day/night [For numbers, see p. 129]	per dag/nacht
	pair duk/nukt

Rented accommodation: problem solving

ESSENTIAL INFORMATION

- If you are looking for accommodation to rent, look out for:
  TE HUUR (for rent)
  APPARTEMENTEN (apartments, rooms)
  KAMERS (rooms)
  VILLA (villa)
  HUIS (house, cottage)
  BUNGALOW (bungalow)
- For arranging details of your rental, see 'Hotel' p. 28.
- Key words you will meet if renting on the spot:
  vooruitbetaling (deposit)
  vor-o-eet-ber-tahling
  sleutel (key)
  slertel
- Having arranged your own accommodation and arrived with the key, check the obvious basics that you take for granted.
  Electricity: Voltage? Razors and small appliances brought from home may need adjusting. You may need an adaptor.
  Gas Town gas or bottled gas? Butane gas must be kept indoors, propane gas must be kept outdoors.
  Stove Don't be surprised to find:
  the grill inside the oven, or no grill at all
  a lid covering the rings which lifts up to form a 'splashback'
  a mixture of two gas rings and two electric rings
  Toilet Mains drainage or septic tank? Don't flush disposable diapers or anything else down the toilet if you are on a septic tank.
  Water Find the stopcock. Check taps and plugs—they may not operate in the way you are used to. Check how to turn on (or light) the hot water.
  Windows Check the method of opening and closing windows and shutters.
  Insects Is an insecticide spray provided? If not, get one locally.
  Equipment See p. 54 for buying or replacing equipment.
  You will probably have an official agent, but be clear in your own mind who to contact in an emergency, even if it is only a neighbour in the first instance.

WHAT TO SAY

My name is . . .	**Mijn naam is . . .** mane nahm is . . .
I'm staying at . . .	**Ik verblijf . . .** ik ver-bleyf . . .
They've cut off . . .	**Ze hebben . . . afgesneden** zer hebben . . . *uf*-her-snaden
the electricity	**de elektriciteit** der ay-lek-tree-see-t*ait*
the gas	**het gas** et hus
the water	**het water** et w*ah*-ter
Is there . . . in the area?	**Is er een . . . in de omgeving?** is er en . . . in der om-*hay*ving
an electrician	**een elektriciën** en ay-lek-tree-see-*en*
a plumber	**een loodgieter** en *loat*-heeter
a gas fitter	**een gasfitter** en h*us*-fitter
Where is . . .	**Waar is . . .** wahr is . . .
the fuse box?	**de zekering?** der z*ay*ker-ring
the stopcock?	**de hoofdkraan?** der h*oaft*-krahn
the boiler?	**de boiler?** der boiler
the geyser?	**de geiser?** de heyser
Is there . . .	**Is er . . .** is er . . .
bottled gas?	**buta-gas?** boota-hus
a septic tank?	**een beerput?** en b*air*-poot
central heating?	**centrale verwarming?** cen-trah-ler ver-w*arming*
The cooker	**Het fornuis** et for-n*o*-ees

The hair dryer	**De haardroger** der *ha*r-dro-*he*r
The heating	**De verwarming** der ver-*wa*rming
The iron	**Het strijkijzer** et str*ey*k-*ey*zer
The pilot light	**De waakvlam** der *wa*hk-vl*u*m
The refrigerator	**De koelkast** der k*oo*l-k*u*st
The telephone	**De telefoon** der tele*fo*ne
The toilet	**Het toilet** et tw*a*h-*le*t
The washing machine	**De wasmachine** der w*u*s-mash*ee*-ner
... is not working	**... werkt niet** ... w*ai*rkt neet
Where can I get ...	**Waar kan ik ... krijgen?** wahr kun ik ... kr*ey*hen
an adaptor for this?	**een hulpstuk voor dit** en h*e*rlp-sterk vor dit
a bottle of butane gas?	**een fles buta-gas** en fles b*oo*ta-hus
a fuse?	**een zekering** en *za*yker-ring
an insecticide spray?	**een insekten-dodende spuitbus** en ins*e*kten-d*o*h-den-der sp*o*-eet-bus
a light bulb?	**een gloeilamp** en hl*oo*y-lump
The drains	**De afvoer** der *u*f-voor
The sink	**De gootsteen** der h*oa*t-stayn
The toilet	**Het toilet** et twah-*le*t
... is blocked	**is verstopt** ... is ver-st*op*t
The gas is leaking	**Het gas lekt** et hus lekt
Can you mend it straightaway?	**Kunt u het direct maken?** koont oo et dee-*re*ct m*a*hken

When can you mend it?	**Wanneer kunt u het maken?**
	wun-nair koont oo et mahken
How much do I owe you?	**Hoeveel is het?**
	hoo-vale is et
When is the rubbish collected?	**Wanneer wordt het vuil opgehaald?**
	wun-nair wort et vo-eel
	op-her-hahlt

LIKELY REACTIONS

What's your name?	**Wat is uw naam?**
	wut is oo nahm
What's your address?	**Wat is uw adres?**
	wut is oo ah-dres
There's a shop ...	**Er is een winkel ...**
	er is en winkel ...
in town	**in de stad**
	in der stut
in the village	**in het dorp**
	in et dorp
I can't come ...	**Ik kan ... niet komen**
	ik kun ... neet koh-men
today	**vandaag**
	vun-dahk
this week	**deze week**
	dazer wake
until Monday	**tot maandag**
	tot mahn-duk
I can come ...	**Ik kan komen ...**
	ik kun koh-men ...
on Tuesday	**op dinsdag**
	op dins-duk
when you want	**wanneer u wilt**
	wun-nair oo wilt
Every day	**Elke dag**
	el-ker duk
Every other day	**Om de andere dag**
	om der un-der-er duk
On Wednesdays	**Op woensdag**
	op woons-duk

[*For days of the week, see p. 133*]

General shopping

The drug store/The chemist's

ESSENTIAL INFORMATION

- Look for the words
  APOTHEEK and **DROGIST**.
  You may also see the following
  signs. A serpent on a staff denotes
  an **apotheek** and a bust of a **gaper**
  (yawner) a **drogist.**
- Medicines (drugs) are available
  only at the **apotheek.**
- Some non-drugs can be bought
  at the **drogist,** at department
  stores or supermarkets.
- Dispensing drug stores are
  open Monday to Friday
  8:00 a.m. – 5:30 p.m.
  Drug stores take it in turn to
  stay open over the weekend
  and at night.
- Some toiletries can also be
  bought at a **PARFUMERIE** and at hairdressing salons.
- Finding a drug store, see p. 20.

WHAT TO SAY

I'd like . . .	**Ik zou graag . . . hebben**
	ik zow hrahk . . . hebben
some Alka Seltzer	**wat Alka Seltzer**
	wut alka seltzer
some antiseptic	**een antiseptisch middel**
	en untee-septees middel
some aspirin	**wat aspirine**
	wut uspee-reener
some bandage	**wat verband**
	wut ver-bunt
some cotton wool	**wat watten**
	wut wutten
some eye drops	**wat oogdruppels**
	wut oak-druppels
some foot powder	**wat voetpoeder**
	wut voot-pooder
some gauze dressing	**wat verbandgaas**
	wut ver-bunt-hahs
some inhalant	**een inhaleermiddel**
	en in-hah-lair-middel
some insect repellent	**een insecten afweermiddel**
	een insecten uf-wair-middel
some lip salve	**wat lippenzalf**
	wut lippen-zulf
some nose drops	**wat neusdruppels**
	wut ners-druppels
some sticking plaster	**wat pleisters**
	wut pley-sters
some throat pastilles	**wat keelpastilles**
	wut kale-pus-til-yes
some vaseline	**wat vaseline**
	wut vah-ser-lee-ner
I'd like something for . . .	**Ik zou graag iets hebben voor . . .**
	ik zow hrahk eets hebben vor . . .
bites	**beten**
	bayten
burns	**brandwonden**
	brunt-wonden
chilblains	**wintervoeten**
	winter-vooten

I'd like something for . . .	Ik zou graag iets hebben voor . . .
	ik zow hrahk eets hebben vor . . .
a cold	verkoudheid
	ver-kowt-hate
constipation	constipatie
	con-stee-pah-tsee
a cough	hoest
	hoost
diarrhoea	diarree
	dee-ar-ray
ear-ache	oorpijn
	or-pain
flu	griep
	hreep
sore gums	zeer tandvlees
	zair tunt-vlays
sprains	verstuikingen
	ver-sto-ee-king-en
stings	steken
	stayken
sunburn	zonnebrand
	zonner-brunt
travel sickness	reis ziekte
	reys zeek-ter
I need . . .	Ik heb . . . nodig
	ik hep . . . nodik
some baby food	wat baby voeding
	wut baby vooding
some contraceptives	wat voorbehoedsmiddelen
	wut vor-ber-hoots-middelen
a deodorant	een deodorant
	en day-oh-doh-runt
some disposable nappies	wat weggooi luiers
	wut wek-hoy lo-ee-ers
some handcream	wat hand creme
	wut hunt crem
some lipstick	een lippenstift
	en lippen-stift
some make-up remover	een make-up remover
	en make-up remover
some paper tissues	wat papieren tissues
	wut pah-pee-ren tis-sues

some razor blades	**wat scheermesjes**
	wut sk*air*-mes-yes
some safety pins	**wat veiligheidsspelden**
	wut *vey*-lik-hates-spelden
some sanitary towels	**wat damesverband**
	wut d*ah*-mes-ver-b*u*nt
some shaving cream	**wat scheerzeep**
	wut sk*air*-zape
some soap	**wat zeep**
	wut zape
some suntan oil/lotion	**wat zonnebrand olie/creme**
	wut *zo*nner-brunt *o*h-lee/crem
some talcum powder	**wat talkpoeder**
	wut tulk-pooder
some Tampax	**wat Tampax**
	wut t*u*mpux
some (soft) toilet paper	**wat (zacht) toiletpapier**
	wut (zukt) twah-l*e*t-pah-peer
some toothpaste	**wat tandpasta**
	wut t*u*nt-pus-tah

[For other essential expressions, see 'Shop talk', p. 56]

Holiday items

ESSENTIAL INFORMATION

● Places to shop at and signs to look for:
  BOEKWINKEL (bookshop, stationery)
  FOTOGRAFIE (films)
  and of course department stores such as:
  DE BIJENKORF
  HEMA
  VROOM EN DREESMANN

WHAT TO SAY

Where can I buy . . . ?	**Waar kan ik . . . kopen?**
	wahr kun ik . . . kopen
I'd like . . .	**Ik zou graag . . .**
	ik zow hrahk . . .
a bag	**een tas**
	en tus
a beach ball	**een strandbal**
	en strunt-bul
a bucket	**een emmer**
	en emmer
an English newspaper	**een engelse krant**
	en eng-el-ser krunt
some envelopes	**wat enveloppen**
	wut enver-loppen
a guide book	**een reisgids**
	en reys-hits
a map (of the area)	**een kaart (van de omgeving)**
	en kart (vun der om-hayving)
some postcards	**wat ansichtkaarten**
	wut unsikt-karten
a spade	**een schop**
	en skop
a straw hat	**een stroohoed**
	en stroh-hoot
a suitcase	**een koffer**
	een koffer

some sunglasses	**een zonnebril**
	en zonner-bril
a sunshade	**een zonnescherm**
	en zonner-sk*ai*rm
an umbrella	**een paraplu**
	en pah-rah-pl*oo*
some writing paper	**wat schrijfpapier**
	wut skr*ey*f-pah-peer
I'd like . . . [*show the camera*]	**Ik zou graag . . . hebben**
	ik z*ow* hr*ah*k . . . hebben
a colour film	**een kleurenfilm**
	en kler-ren-film
a black and white film	**een zwart-wit film**
	en zwart-wit film
for prints	**voor afdrukken**
	vor *u*f-drukken
for slides	**voor dia's**
	vor dee-ahs
12 (24/36) exposures	**twaalf (vierentwintig/zesendertig)**
	opnamen
	twahlf (v*ee*r-en-twintik/
	zes-en-dairtik) *op*-nahmen
a standard 8mm film	**een normaal acht millimeter film**
	en norm*ah*l ukt mili-m*ay*ter film
a super 8 film	**een super acht film**
	en s*oo*per ukt film
some flash bulbs	**een paar flitslampen**
	en par fl*i*ts-lumpen
This camera is broken	**Deze camera is kapot**
	d*a*zer k*ah*mera is kah-p*o*t
The film is stuck	**De film zit vast**
	der film zit vust
Please can you . . .	**Kunt u dit . . . alstublieft?**
	koont oo dit . . . uls-too-bl*ee*ft
develop/print this?	**ontwikkelen/afdrukken**
	ont-wikkelen/*u*f-drerkken
Please can you load the camera for me?	**Kunt u de film in de camera doen alstublieft?**
	koont oo der film in der k*ah*mera doon uls-too-bl*ee*ft

[*For other essential expressions, see 'Shop talk' p. 56*]

The smoke shop

ESSENTIAL INFORMATION

- Tobacco is sold where you see these signs: **TABAKSWINKEL** or **SIGARENHANDEL**.
- To ask if there is one near by, see p. 20.
- Most usual brands of tobacco, cigars and cigarettes may be bought at supermarkets and station restaurants.

WHAT TO SAY

A packet of cigarettes . . .	**Een pakje sigaretten . . .**
	en p*u*k-yer see-hah-retten . . .
with filters	**met filter**
	m*e*t filter
without filters	**zonder filter**
	z*o*nder filter
king size	**king size**
	king size
menthol	**menthol**
	ment*o*l
Those up there . . .	**Die daar boven . . .**
	dee dar b*o*ven . . .
on the right	**rechts**
	r*e*kts
on the left	**links**
	links
These [*point*]	**Deze**
	d*a*zer
Cigarettes, please	**Sigaretten, alstublieft**
	see-hah-retten uls-too-bl*ee*ft
100, 200, 300	**honderd, twee honderd, drie honderd**
	h*o*ndert, tway h*o*ndert, dree hondert
Two packets	**Twee pakjes**
	tway p*u*k-yes

Have you got. . .	**Heeft u. . .**
	hayft oo. . .
English cigarettes?	**engelse sigaretten?**
	eng-elser see-hah-retten
American cigarettes?	**amerikaanse sigaretten?**
	ah-may-ree-kahn-ser see-hah-retten
English pipe tobacco?	**engelse pijptabak?**
	eng-elser pape-tah-buk
American pipe tobacco?	**amerikaanse pijptabak?**
	ah-may-ree-kahn-ser pape-tah-buk
rolling tobacco?	**shag?**
	shek
A packet of pipe tobacco	**Een pakje pijptabak**
	en puk-yer pape-tah-buk
That one down there . . .	**Die daar beneden . . .**
	dee dar ber-nayden . . .
on the right	**rechts**
	rekts
on the left	**links**
	links
This one [point]	**Deze**
	dazer
A cigar, please	**Een sigaar, alstublieft**
	en see-har uls-too-bleeft
Some cigars, please	**Een paar sigaren, alstublieft**
	en par see-hah-ren uls-too-bleeft
Those [point]	**Die**
	dee
A box of matches	**Een doosje lucifers**
	en dohs-yer loo-see-fairs
A packet of pipe cleaners	**Een pakje pijperagers**
[show lighter]	en puk-yer paper-rah-hers
A packet of flints	**Een pakje vuursteentjes**
	en puk-yer voor-staynt-yers
Lighter fuel	**Benzine**
	ben-zeener
Lighter gas, please	**Aansteker gas, alstublieft**
	ahn-stay-ker hus uls-too-bleeft

[For other essential expressions, see 'Shop talk' p. 56]

Buying clothes

ESSENTIAL INFORMATION

- Look for:
    DAMESKLEDING (women's clothes)
    HERENKLEDING (men's clothes)
    KINDERKLEDING (children's clothes)
    SCHOENENWINKEL (shoe shop)
- Don't buy without being measured first or without trying things on.
- Don't rely on conversion charts of clothing sizes [see p. 145].
- If you are buying for someone else, take their measurements with you.

WHAT TO SAY

I'd like . . .	**Ik zou graag . . . hebben**
	ik zow hrahk . . . hebben
an anorak	**een anorak**
	en *ah*-noh-ruk
a belt	**een riem**
	en reem
a bikini	**een bikini**
	en bikini
a bra	**een BH**
	en bay-hah
a pair of briefs	**een damesbroekje**
	en d*ah*-mes-br*oo*k-yer
a cap (swimming)	**een badmuts**
	en b*u*t-merts
a cap (skiing)	**een skimuts**
	en sk*ee*-merts
a cardigan	**een vest**
	en vest
a coat	**een mantel**
	en m*u*ntel
a dress	**een jurk**
	en yerk
a hat	**een hoed**
	en hoot

a jacket	een jasje
	en yus-yer
a pair of jeans	een spijkerbroek
	en speyker-brook
a jumper	een jumper
	en yum-per
a nightdress	een nachtjapon
	en nukt-yah-pon
a pullover	een pullover
	een pullover
a pair of pyjamas	een pyjama
	en pee-yah-mah
a raincoat	een regenjas
	en ray-hen-yus
a shirt	een overhemd
	en over-hemt
a pair of shorts	shorts
	shorts
a skirt	een rok
	en rok
a suit	een pak
	en puk
a swimsuit	een badpak
	en but-puk
a tee-shirt	een T-shirt
	en tee-shirt
a pair of tights	een mayot
	en mah-yo
a pair of trousers	een broek
	een brook
a pair of underpants	een onderbroek
	en onder-brook
I'd like a pair of . . .	Ik zou graag een paar . . . hebben
	ik zow hrahk en par . . . hebben
gloves	handschoenen
	hunt-skoonen
socks (short/long)	sokken (kort/lang)
	sokken (kort/lung)
stockings	kousen
	kow-sen

I'd like a pair of . . .	Ik zou graag een paar . . . hebben
	ik zow hrahk een par . . . hebben
shoes	schoenen
	skoonen
canvas shoes	linnen schoenen
	linnen skoonen
sandals	sandalen
	sun-dahlen
beach shoes	strandschoenen
	strunt-skoonen
smart shoes	geklede schoenen
	her-klayder skoonen
boots	laarzen
	larzen
moccasins	mocassin
	mok-kus-sin
My size is . . .	Mijn maat is . . .
[For numbers, see p. 129]	mane maht is . . .
Can you measure me, please?	Kunt u me meten, alstublieft?
	koont oo mer mayten uls-too-bleeft
Can I try it on?	Mag ik het aanpassen?
	muk ik et ahn-pussen
It's for a present	Het is voor een cadeau
	et is vor en kah-do
These are the measurements . . .	Dit zijn de maten . . .
[show written]	dit zane der mahten . . .
bust/chest	borst
	borst
collar	kraag
	krahk
hip	heup
	herp
leg	been
	bayn
waist	taille
	tye-yer

Have you got something . . .	Heeft u iets . . .
	hayft oo eets . . .
in black?	in zwart?
	in zwart
in white?	in wit?
	in wit
in grey?	in grijs?
	in hreys
in blue?	in blauw?
	in bla-oo
in brown?	in bruin?
	in bro-een
in pink?	in roze?
	in rohs
in green?	in groen?
	in hroon
in red?	in rood?
	in rote
in yellow?	in geel?
	in hale
in this colour? [point]	in deze kleur?
	in dazer kler
in cotton?	in katoen?
	in kah-toon
in denim?	in keper?
	in kayper
in leather?	in leer?
	in lair
in nylon?	in nylon?
	in ney-lon
in suede	in suède?
	in soo-ay-der
in wool?	in wol?
	in wol
in this material? [point]	in dit materiaal?
	in dit mah-teree-ahl

[For other essential expressions, see 'Shop talk', p. 56]

Replacing equipment

ESSENTIAL INFORMATION

- Look for these shops and signs:
  IJZERHANDEL/IJZERWAREN (hardware)
  ELEKTRICITEITSWINKEL (electrical goods)
  HUISHOUDARTIKELEN (household articles)
- In a supermarket look for this display:
  ONDERHOUDSARTIKELEN (household cleaning materials).
- To ask the way to the shop, see p. 20.
- At a campsite try their shop first.

WHAT TO SAY

Have you got . . .	Heeft u . . .
	hayft oo . . .
an adaptor?	een hulpstuk?
[show appliance]	en herlp-sterk
a bottle of butane gas?	een fles buta-gas?
	en fles boota-hus
a bottle of propane gas?	een fles propaan gas?
	en fles pro-pahn hus
a bottle opener?	een flesopener?
	en fles-opener
a corkscrew?	een kurketrekker?
	en ker-ker-trekker
any disinfectant?	een ontsmettingsmiddel?
	en ont-smettings-middel
any disposable cups?	wat weggooikoppen?
	wut wek-hoy-koppen
a drying-up cloth?	een theedoek?
	en tay-dook
any forks?	een paar vorken?
	en par vorken
a fuse? [show old one]	een zekering?
	en zayker-ring
an insecticide spray?	een insektendodend middel?
	en insekten-dohdent middel
a paper kitchen roll?	een papieren keukenrol?
	en pah-pee-ren ker-ken-rol

any knives?*	**een paar messen?**
	en par messen
a light bulb? [show old one]	**een gloeilampje?**
	en hlooy-lump-yer
a plastic bucket?	**een plastieken emmer?**
	en plus-teeken emmer
a plastic can?	**een plastieken kan?**
	en plus-teeken kun
a scouring pad?	**een pannespons?**
	en punner-spons
a spanner?	**een moersleutel?**
	en moor-slertel
a sponge?	**een spons?**
	en spons
any string?	**wat touw?**
	wut tow
any tent pegs?	**een paar tentpennen?**
	en par tent-pennen
a tin opener?	**een blikopener?**
	en blik-opener
a torch?	**een zaklantaarn?**
	en zuk-lun-tarn
any torch batteries?	**een paar zaklantaarn batterijen?**
	en par zuk-luñ-tarn butter-rey-en
a universal plug (for the sink)?	**een algemene stop (voor de gootsteen)?**
	en ulher-mayner stop (vor der hoat-stayn
a washing line?	**een waslijn?**
	en wus-lane
any washing powder?	**wat waspoeder?**
	wut wus-pooder
a washing-up brush?	**een afwasborstel?**
	en ufwus-borstel
any washing-up liquid?	**een vloeibaar afwasmiddel?**
	en vlooy-bar ufwus-middel

[For other essential expressions, see 'Shop talk', p. 56.]

Shop talk

ESSENTIAL INFORMATION

- Know your coins and bills
  coins: the guilder is divided into 100 cents. Some of these coins have 'popular' names; 5 cents **een stuiver**, 10 cents **een dubbeltje**, 25 cents **een kwartje**, Fl. 2.50 **een rijksdaalder**
  bills Fl. 5, Fl. 10, Fl. 25, Fl. 1000
- Know how to say the important weights and measures. You will hear grams, ounces, kilos and pounds used in shops and markets. The metric Dutch pound **pond** (pont) is ten per cent more than the UK pound and there are exactly **2 pond** in 1 kilo. The metric Dutch ounce **ons** (ons) is equivalent to 100 grams. Throughout the book you will find that we have used the colloquial Dutch expressions (i.e. ½ oz, 1 oz, 1 lb) to translate grams and kilograms, as they are both more widely used and simpler to say.
  [For numbers, see p. 129]
- Coins: 5 cents, 10 cents, 25 cents, Fl. 1, Fl. 2.50, Fl. 5
  Bills: Fl. 10, Fl. 25, Fl. 50, Fl. 250, Fl. 1000

CURRENCY CONVERTER

● Since the relative strengths of currencies vary, it is not possible to provide accurate exchange rates here. However, by filling in the charts below prior to your trip, you can create a handy currency converter.

Dollars	Guilders
1	
2	
3	
4	
5	
10	
15	
25	
50	
75	
100	
250	

Guilders	Dollars
1	
2	
3	
4	
5	
10	
15	
25	
50	
75	
100	
250	
500	

50 grams/½ oz	**vijftig gram/een half ons**
	v*e*yftik hrum/en hulf ons
100 grams/1 oz	**honderd gram/één ons**
	h*o*ndert hrum/ayn ons
200 grams/2 oz	**tweehonderd gram/twee ons**
	tway-hondert hrum/tway ons
250 grams/½ lb	**tweehonderdvijftig gram/een half pond**
	tway-hondert-v*e*yftik hrum/en hulf pont
½ kilo/1 lb	**een halve kilo/één pond**
	en h*u*lver kilo/ayn pont
1 kilo/2 lbs	**één kilo/twee pond**
	ayn kilo/tway pont
2 kilos	**twee kilo**
	tway kilo
½ litre	**een halve liter**
	een h*u*lver l*ee*ter
1 litre	**één liter**
	ayn l*ee*ter
2 litres	**twee liter**
	tway l*ee*ter

● In small shops don't be surprised if customers, as well as the shop assistant say 'hello' and 'goodbye' to you.

CUSTOMER

Hello	**Hallo**
	hull*o*
Good morning	**Goede morgen**
	h*oo*-der mor-hen
Good afternoon	**Goede middag**
	h*oo*-der m*i*d-duk
Goodbye	**Tot ziens**
	tot z*ee*ns
I'm just looking	**Ik kijk even**
	ik keyk *a*y-ven
Excuse me	**Excuseer me**
	ex-coo-s*ai*r mer
How much is this/that?	**Hoeveel is dit/dat?**
	h*oo*-vale is dit/dut

What's that?	**Wat is dat?**
	wut is dut
What are those?	**Wat zijn dat?**
	wut zane dut
Is there a discount?	**Is er korting op?**
	is er korting op
I'd like that, please	**Ik wil dat graag hebben, alstublieft**
	ik wil dut hrahk hebben uls-too-bleeft
Not that	**Dat niet**
	dut neet
Like that	**Zoals dat**
	zo-uls dut
That's enough, thank you	**Dat is genoeg, dank u**
	dut is her-nook dunk oo
More please	**Wat meer alstublieft**
	wut mair uls-too-bleeft
Less please	**Wat minder alstublieft**
	wut min-der uls-too-bleeft
That's fine	**Dat is fijn**
	dut is fane
OK	**OK**
	okay
I won't take it, thank you	**Ik neem het niet, dank u**
	ik name et neet dunk oo
It's not right	**Het is niet goed**
	et is neet hoot
Thank you very much	**Dank u wel**
	dunk oo wel
Have you got something . . .	**Heeft u iets . . .**
	heyft oo eets . . .
better?	beters?
	bayters
cheaper?	goedkopers?
	hoot-kopers
different?	anders?
	unders
larger?	groters?
	hroh-ters
smaller?	kleiners?
	kleyners

At what time do you . . .	Hoe laat gaat u . . .
	hoo laht haht oo . . .
open?	open?
	*o*pen
close?	dicht?
	dikt
Can I have a bag, please?	Mag ik een zak, alstublieft?
	muk ik en *zu*k uls-too-bl*ee*ft
Can I have a receipt?	Mag ik een kwitantie?
	muk ik en kv. ee-tun-tsee
Do you take . . .	Neemt u . . . aan?
	naymt oo . . . ahn
English/American money?	engels/amerikaans geld
	*e*ng-els/ah-may-ree-k*a*hns helt
travellers' cheques?	reischeques
	r*e*ys-cheques
credit cards?	credietkaarten
	cred*ee*t-karten
I'd like . . .	Ik zou graag . . .
	ik zow hrahk . . .
one like that	één zoals dat
	ayn zo-uls dut
two like that	twee zoals dat
	tway zo-uls dut

SHOP ASSISTANT

Can I help you?	**Kan ik u helpen?** kun ik oo helpen
What would you like?	**Wat wilt u hebben?** wut wilt oo hebben
Will that be all?	**Is dat alles?** is dut ul-les
Anything else?	**Iets anders?** eets unders
Would you like it wrapped?	**Wilt u het ingepakt hebben?** wilt oo et in-her-pukt hebben
Sorry, none left	**Tot mijn spijt, uitverkocht** tot mane spate o-eet-ver-kokt
I haven't got any	**Ik heb geen** ik heb hane
I haven't got any more	**Ik heb geen meer** ik hep hane mair
How many do you want?⎤ How much do you want?⎦ Is this enough?	**Hoeveel wenst u?** hoo-vale wenst oo **Is dit genoeg?** is dit her-nook

Shopping for food

Bread

ESSENTIAL INFORMATION

- Finding a baker's, see p. 18.
- Key words to look for:
  BAKKERIJ (baker's)
  BAKKER (baker)
  BROOD (bread)
- Supermarkets of any size and general stores nearly always sell bread.
- Opening times are usually 8.30 a.m. – 5.30 p.m.; early closing time varies slightly locally.
- The most characteristic type of loaf is the 'French stick', which comes in two sizes: large and small.
- Most bread is sold unsliced in both bakeries and supermarkets. However, if you prefer your bread sliced gesneden (her-snayden), hand the loaf to the assistant and she will slice it for you. You will have to pay a small charge for this service.

WHAT TO SAY

A loaf (like that)	**Een brood (zoals dat)**
	en brote (zo-uls dut)
A whole loaf	**Een heel brood**
	en hale brote
A half loaf	**Een half brood**
	en hulf brote
A white loaf	**Een wit brood**
	en wit brote
A wholemeal loaf	**Een tarwe brood**
	en tar-wer brote
A currant loaf	**Een krentenbrood**
	en krenter-brote
A packet of pumpernickel	**Een pakje roggebrood**
	en puk-yer rok-her-brote
A bread roll	**Een broodje**
	een brote-yer
A currant bun	**Een krentenbol**
	en krenter-bol
Two loaves	**Twee broden**
	tway broden
Three rolls	**Drie broodjes**
	dree brote-yers
Four currant buns	**Vier krentenbollen**
	veer krenter-bollen
Two packets of rusks	**Twee rollen beschuit**
	tway rollen ber-sko-eet
A French stick	**Een stokbrood**
	en stok-brote

[*For other essential expressions, see 'Shop talk' p. 56*]

Cakes

ESSENTIAL INFORMATION

- Key words to look for:
  BANKETBAKKERIJ (cake shop)
  BANKETBAKKER (cake/pastry maker)
  GEBAK (pastries/cakes)
- To find a cake shop, see p. 20.
- **THEE-SALON**: a place to buy cakes and have a drink, usually in the afternoon. See also p. 82 'Ordering a drink'.

WHAT TO SAY

The type of cakes you find in the shops may vary from region to region but the following are the most common; cake is *not* bought per slice, but gâteau is.

een cake	a plain butter cake; size about
en cake	300 – 700 grams
een rozijnen cake	a raisin cake
en roh-zeynen cake	
een citroen cake	a lemon cake
en citroon cake	
een appeltaart	an apple tart
en uppel-tart	
een slagroomtaart	a cream tart/gâteau
en sluk-rome-tart	
een vruchtentaart	a fruit tart/gâteau
en vrukten-tart	
een kwarktaart	a cheese (cream) cake/gâteau
en kwark-tart	
roomsoezen	éclairs
rome-soozen	
slagroomgebakjes	cream pastries
sluk-rome-her-buk-yers	
vruchtengebakjes	fruit pastries
vrukten-her-buk-yers	
amandelbroodjes	almond rolls
um-mundel-brote-yers	

Medium-size cakes and pastries are usually bought by number:

One almond roll, please **Eén amandelbroodje, alstublieft**
                          ayn um-mundel-brote-yer
                          uls-too-bleeft

Two almond rolls, please **Twee amandelbroodjes, alstublieft**
                          tway um-mundel-brote-yers
                          uls-too-bleeft

Biscuits are bought by weight:

200 grams of biscuits **Twee ons koekjes**
                       tway ons kook-yers

250 grams mixed biscuits **Een half pond gemengde koekjes**
                          en hulf pont her-meng-der kook-
                          yers

[For further details on Dutch weights, see 'Shop talk', p. 56]

You may want to buy a larger cake by the slice:

One slice of apple cake **Eén punt appelgebak**
                         ayn pernt uppel-her-buk

Two slices of cheesecake **Twee punten kwarktaart**
                          tway pern-ten kwark-tart

You may also say:

A selection, please **Wat gebak, alstublieft**
                     wut her-buk uls-too-bleeft

[For other essential expressions, see 'Shop talk', p. 56]

Ice-cream and sweets

ESSENTIAL INFORMATION

- Key words to look for:
  IJS (ice-cream)
  IJS-SALON (ice-cream parlour)
  BONBONS en CHOCOLADE (chocolates)
  BANKETBAKKERIJ (pastry maker's)
  BANKETBAKKER (pastry maker)
  SUIKERWERKEN (sweet shop)
- Best known ice-cream brand-names are:
  OLA
  CAMPINA
  CARACA
  VENEZIA
- When buying ice-cream, specify what price cone or tub you want.
- Pre-packed sweets are available in general stores and supermarkets.

WHAT TO SAY

A ... ice, please	Een ... ijsje, alstublieft
	en ... eys-yer uls-too-bleeft
banana	bananen
	bah-nah-nen
chocolate	chocolade
	shocolah-der
mocha	mokka
	mokka
pistachio	pistache
	peestush
strawberry	aardbeien
	ard-bey-yen
vanilla	vanille
	vun-il-yer
One (50 cent) cone	Eén van (vijftig)
	ayn vun (veyftik)
Two (Fl. 1) cones	Twee van (één gulden)
	tway vun (ayn hoolden)

Two (Fl. 1.50) tubs	Twee bekertjes van (één vijftig)
	tway bakert-yes vun (ayn veyftik)
A lollipop	Een lollie
	en lollee
A packet of ...	Een pakje ...
	en puk-yer ...
100 grams of ...	Eén ons ...
	ayn ons ...
200 grams of ...	Twee ons ...
	tway ons ...

[*For further details of Dutch weights, see 'Shop talk', p. 56*]

chewing gum	**kauw gom**
	cow hom
chocolates	**bonbons**
	bonbons
liquorice	**dropjes**
	drop-yers
mints	**pepermunt**
	paper-munt
sweets	**snoepjes**
	snoop-yers
toffees	**toffees**
	toffays

[*For other essential expressions, see 'Shop talk' p. 56*]

In the supermarket

ESSENTIAL INFORMATION
- The place to ask for: [*see p. 20*]
  EEN SUPERMARKT (supermarket)
  EEN KRUIDENIERSWINKEL (grocery shop)
- Key instructions on signs in the shop:
  INGANG (entrance)   KASSA (cash desk)
  UITGANG (exit)   RECLAME (on offer)
  GEEN INGANG (no entry)   ZELFBEDIENING (self-service)
  GEEN UITGANG (no exit)
- Opening times vary but in general are weekdays between 8.30/
  9.00 a.m. – 5.30/6.00 p.m., and Saturdays 8.30/9.00 a.m. – 4.00
  p.m. Some shops have introduced late closing and you will find
  that others are closed during lunchtime.
- No need to say anything in a supermarket, but ask if you can't
  see what you want.
- For non-food items see 'Replacing equipment', p. 54.

WHAT TO SAY

Excuse me, please	Pardon
	pardon
Where is . . .	Waar is . . .
	wahr is . . .
the bread?	het brood?
	et brote
the butter?	de boter?
	der boter
the cheese?	de kaas?
	der kahs
the chocolate?	de chocolade?
	der shocolah-der
the coffee?	de koffie?
	der coffee
the cooking oil?	de kookolie?
	der coke-oh-lee
the fish?	de vis?
	der vis
the frozen food?	het diepvries voedsel?
	et deep-frees vootsel
the fruit?	het fruit?
	et fro-eet

the jam?	**de jam?**
	der shem
the meat?	**het vlees?**
	et vlays
the milk?	**de melk?**
	der melk
the mineral water?	**het mineraal water?**
	et mee-ner-*r*ahl *w*ah-ter
the salt?	**het zout?**
	et zowt
the sugar?	**de suiker?**
	der so-ee-ker
the tea?	**de thee?**
	der tay
the vinegar?	**de azijn?**
	der ah-zeyn
the wine?	**de wijn?**
	der weyn
the yogurt?	**de yoghurt?**
	der yo-hurt
Where are . . .	**Waar zijn . . .**
	wahr zane . . .
the biscuits?	**de koekjes?**
	der kook-yers
the crisps?	**de chips?**
	der chips
the eggs?	**de eieren?**
	der ey-er-en
the fruit juices?	**de vruchtensappen?**
	der vrukten-suppen
the pastas?	**de meelsoorten?**
	der mail-sorten
the soft drinks?	**de frisdranken?**
	der fris-drunken
the sweets?	**de snoepjes?**
	der snoop-yers
Where are . . .	**Waar is . . .**
	wahr is . . .
the tinned vegetables?	**de blikgroente?**
	der blik-hroonter
the vegetables?	**de groente?**
	der hroonter

[For other essential expressions, see 'Shop talk' p. 56]

Picnic food

ESSENTIAL INFORMATION

● Key words to look for:
  DELICATESSEN ⎤ delicatessen
  VLEESWAREN ⎦
  Weight guide: 150 grams of prepared salad per two people, if
  eaten as a starter to a substantial meal; 100 grams of prepared
  salad per person, if to be eaten as the main part of a picnic-type
  meal.

WHAT TO SAY

A slice of . . .	Een plak . . .
	en pluk . . .
Two slices of . . .	Twee plakken . . .
	tway plukken . . .
roast beef	rosbief
	ros-beef
roast pork	varkens rollade
	var-kens rollah-der
tongue	tong
	tong
ham	ham
	hum
liver sausage	leverworst
	layver-worst
garlic sausage	knoflook worst
	knof-loke worst
salami	salami
	sah-lah-mee
100 grams of . . .	Eén ons . . .
	ayn ons . . .
150 grams of . . .	Anderhalf ons . . .
	under-hulf ons . . .
200 grams of . . .	Twee ons . . .
	tway ons . . .
300 grams of . . .	Drie ons . . .
	dree ons . . .

[For further details of Dutch weights, see 'Shop talk' p. 56]

potato salad	**aardappelsla**
	ar-duppel-slah
herring salad	**haring sla**
	hah-ring slah
Russian salad	**huzaren sla**
	hoo-*zah*-ren slah
coleslaw	**koolsla**
	kohl-slah
olives	**olijven**
	oh-*ley*-ven

You might also like to try some of these:

een stuk rookworst	a piece of smoked sausage (best
en sterk *roke*-worst	eaten hot)
een zoute nieuwe haring	a salted fresh herring
en *zowter nee*-wer *hah*ring	
een gerookte paling	a smoked eel
en her-*roke*-ter *pah*-ling	
een Frankfurter	a Frankfurter sausage
en fr*unk*-foorter	
een stuk boterhammenworst	some luncheon meat
en sterk *boter*-hummer-worst	
wat rookvlees	some smoked beef (thin, salty
wut *roke*-vlays	slices)
wat gerookte makreel	some smoked mackerel
wut her-*roke*-ter m*ah*-krayl	
wat zult	some brawn: pork (boar's flesh)
wut zult	pickled in vinegar
wat vis-sla	some fish salad
wut *vis*-slah	
wat champignon-sla	some mushroom salad
wut shum-peen-*yon*-slah	
wat gehakt	cold, spicy minced meat (pork or
wut her-h*ukt*	beef)
wat worstsla	some sausage salad
wut *worst*-slah	
wat kippesla	some chicken salad
wut *kipper*-slah	
wat kaassla	some cheese salad
wut *kahs*-slah	
Goudse kaas (belegen)	Gouda cheese (mature)
howtser kahs (berl*ay*-hen)	

Edammer kaas ay-du*mm*er kahs	Edam cheese
Leidse kaas leyt-ser kahs	Leiden cheese (cumin seed cheese)
nagelkaas n*ah*-hel kahs	clove cheese
Limburgse kaas *l*imburg-ser kahs	Limburger (piquant) cheese

Fruit and vegetables

ESSENTIAL INFORMATION

- Key words to look for:
  FRUIT (fruit)
  FRUITHANDELAAR (fruiterer)
  GROENTEN (vegetables)
- If possible, buy fruit and vegetables in the market, where they are cheaper and fresher than in the shops. Open-air markets are held once a week in most areas, usually in the mornings.
- It is customary for you to choose your own fruit and vegetables at the market and for the stallholder to weigh and price them. You must take your own shopping bag as paper and plastic bags are not normally provided.
- Weight guide: 1 kilo of potatoes is sufficient for six people for one meal.

  [*For further details of Dutch weights, see 'Shop talk', p. 56*]

WHAT TO SAY

1/2 kilo of ...	Eén pond ... ayn pont ...
1 kilo of ...	Eén kilo ... ayn k*i*lo ...
2 kilos of ...	Twee kilo ... tway k*i*lo ...
apples	appels *u*ppels

apricots	**abrikozen**
	ah-bree-k*o*zen
bananas	**bananen**
	bah-n*a*h-nen
bilberries	**bosbessen**
	b*o*s-bess*en*
cherries	**kersen**
	k*ai*rsen
grapes (white/black)	**druiven (witte/zwarte)**
	dr*o*-ee-ven (w*i*tter/zw*a*rter)
greengages	**reineclaudes**
	rayner-cl*o*wdes
mulberries	**moerbeien**
	m*oo*r-bey-en
oranges	**sinaasappels**
	see-nahs-uppels
pears	**peren**
	p*a*yren
peaches	**perziken**
	p*ai*rzi-ken
plums	**pruimen**
	pro-ee-men
raspberries	**frambozen**
	frum-b*o*zen
strawberries	**aardbeien**
	*a*rd-bey-yen
A pineapple, please	**Een ananas, alstublieft**
	en *u*n-ah-nus uls-too-bl*ee*ft
A grapefruit	**Een grapefruit**
	en grape-fruit
A melon	**Een meloen**
	en mer-l*oo*n
A water melon	**Een watermeloen**
	en w*a*h-ter-mer-l*oo*n
250 grams of ...	**Een half pond ...**
	en hulf pont ...
1/2 kilo of ...	**Eén pond ...**
	ayn pont ...
1 kilo of ...	**Eén kilo ...**
	ayn k*i*lo ...

1½ kilos of . . .	Anderhalve kilo . . .
	under-hulver kilo . . .

[*For further details of Dutch weights, see 'Shop talk' p. 56*]

aubergines	aubergines
	oh-ber-sheens
broad beans	tuinbonen
	to-een-bonen
carrots	wortels
	wor-tels
green beans	slabonen
	slah-bonen
leeks	prei
	prey
mushrooms	champignons
	shum-peen-yons
onions	uien
	owe-yen
peas	doperwten
	dopair-ten
podded peas	peultjes
	perlt-yers
potatoes	aardappels
	ar-duppels
red cabbage	rode kool
	roder kohl
shallots	sjalotten
	shah-lot-ten
spinach	spinazie
	spee-nah-zee
tomatoes	tomaten
	toh-mah-ten
A bunch of . . .	Een bosje . . .
	en bos-yer . . .
parsley	peterselie
	pa-ter-saylee
radishes	radijs
	rah-deys
A garlic	Een knoflook
	en knof-loke
A lettuce	Een krop sla
	en krop slah
A stick of celery	Een bleekselderij
	en blake-selder-rey

A cauliflower	Een bloemkool
	en bloom-kohl
A cabbage	Een kool
	en kohl
A cucumber	Een komkommer
	en kom-kommer
A turnip	Een witte raap
	en witter rahp
Like that, please	Zoals dat, alstublieft
	zo-uls dut uls-too-bleeft

Vegetables and fruit which may not be familiar:

andijvie un-dey-vee	endive, a salad plant with a bitter flavour
Brussels lof brussels lof	chicory, used in winter salads, same family as the above
knolselderij knol-selder-rey	celeriac, a variety of celery
postelein pos-ter-leyn	purslane, a salad herb

[For other essential expressions, see 'Shop talk' p. 56]

Meat

ESSENTIAL INFORMATION

- Key words to look for:
  SLAGERIJ (butcher's)
  SLAGER (butcher)
- Weight guide: 125–200 grams of meat per person for one meal.
  The diagrams below are to help you make sense of labels on
  counters, windows and supermarket displays, and decide which
  cut or joint to have. Translations don't help, and you don't need
  to say the Dutch word involved.
- Lamb and mutton are expensive in Holland.

WHAT TO SAY

For a joint, choose the type of meat and then say how many people
it is for:

Some beef, please	**Wat rundvlees, alstublieft**
	wut *r*unt-vlays uls-too-bl*eef*t
Some lamb	**Wat lamsvlees**
	wut l*u*ms-vlays
Some mutton	**Wat schapevlees**
	wut skah-per-vlays
Some pork	**Wat varkensvlees**
	wut v*a*rkens-vlays
Some veal	**Wat kalfsvlees**
	wut k*u*lfs-vlays
A joint ...	**Groot stuk vlees ...**
	hrote sterk vlays ...
for two people	**voor twee personen**
	vor tway pair-s*o*hnen
for four people	**voor vier personen**
	vor veer pair-s*o*hnen
for six people	**voor zes personen**
	vor zes pair-s*o*hnen

For steak, liver and kidneys do as above:

Some steak, please	**Wat biefstuk, alstublieft**
	wut b*ee*f-sterk uls-too-bl*ee*ft

Beef Rund

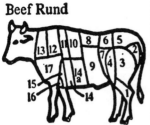

1 Achterschenkel
2 Muis
3 Platte bil
4 Spierstuk
5 Staartstuk
6 Dikke lende
7 Liesstuk
   (ezeltje)
8 Dunne lende
9 Vang
10 Fijne rib
11 Dikke rib
12 Onderrib
13 Hals
14 Naborst
14a Dunne borst
15 Borst
16 Puntborst
17 Schouder met
   voorschenkel

Veal Kalf

1 Achterschenkel
2 Platte fricandeau met staartstuk
2a Dikke lende
3 Kalkoenstuk met liesstuk
4 Lende met vang
   (nierstuk en koteletten)
5 Ribstuk (fijne rib) (koteletten)
6 Ribstuk (dikke rib)
7 Onderrib met hals
8 Dunne borst
9 Borst
10 Schouder met voorschenkel

Pork Varken

1 Ham (vleeskant)
2 Rugspek
3 Buik (mager spek met broek)
4 Schouder
5 Kop met kinnebak

Lamb Lam

1 Bout met been
2 Lamszadel
3 Lamsrug
4 Lamsborst
5 Schouder
6 Nek

Some liver	**Wat lever**
	wut *layver*
Some kidneys	**Wat nieren**
	wut *nee*-ren
Some sausages	**Wat worst**
	wut worst
for three people	**voor drie personen**
	vor dree pair-*sohnen*
for five people	**voor vijf personen**
	vor veyf pair-*sohnen*

For chops do it this way:

Two veal escalopes	**Twee kalfsoesters**
	tway k*u*lfs-oosters
Three pork chops	**Drie varkenskarbonaden**
	dree v*a*rkens-karboh-*nah*den
Four mutton chops	**Vier schaapskarbonaden**
	veer sk*ah*ps-karboh-*nah*den
Five lamb chops	**Vijf lamskarbonaden**
	veyf l*u*ms-karboh-*nah*den

You may also want:

A chicken	**Een kip**
	en kip
A rabbit	**Een konijn**
	en koh-neyn
A tongue	**Een tong**
	en tong

Other essential expressions [*see also p. 56*]

Please can you ...	**Kunt u het ... alstublieft**
	koont oo et ... uls-too-bl*eef*t
mince it?	**malen**
	m*a*hlen
dice it?	**tot dobbelstenen snijden**
	tot d*o*bbel-staynen sn*ey*-den
trim the fat?	**vet afsnijden**
	vet *u*f-sn*ey*-den

Fish

ESSENTIAL INFORMATION

- The place to ask for: EEN VISWINKEL (a fishmonger's)
- Markets and large supermarkets usually have fresh fish stalls. Weight guide 250 grams minimum per person, for one meal, of fish bought on the bone.

  i.e. 1/2 kilo/500 grams for 2 people

     1 kilo for 4 people

     1½ kilos for 6 people

WHAT TO SAY

Purchase large fish and small shellfish by weight:

½ kilo of . . .	Eén pond . . .
	ayn pont . . .
1 kilo of . . .	Eén kilo . . .
	ayn kilo . . .
1½ kilos of . . .	Anderhalve kilo . . .
	under-hulver kilo . . .
cod	kabeljauw
	kahbel-yow
eel	paling
	pahling
haddock	schelvis
	skelvis
herring	haring
	hah-ring
pike	snoek
	snook
plaice	schol
	skol
turbot	tarbot
	tarbot
mussels	mosselen
	mossel-en
prawns	garnalen
	har-nahlen
shrimps	kleine garnalen
	kleyner har-nahlen

Some large fish can be purchased by the slice:

One slice of ...	**Eén moot ...**
	ayn mote ...
Two slices of ...	**Twee moten ...**
	tway moten ...
Six slices of ...	**Zes moten ...**
	zes moten ...
salmon	**zalm**
	zulm
cod	**kabeljauw**
	kahbel-yow
haddock	**schelvis**
	skelvis
tuna	**tonijn**
	toh-neyn

For some shellfish and 'frying pan' fish specify
the number you want:

A crab, please	**Een krab, alstublieft**
	en krup uls-too-bleeft
A lobster	**Een zeekreeft**
	en zay-krayft
A scallop	**Een kammossel**
	en kum-mossel
A plaice	**Een schol**
	en skol
A whiting	**Een wijting**
	en waiting
A trout	**Een forel**
	en foh-rel
A sole	**Een tong**
	en tong
A mackerel	**Een makreel**
	en mah-krayl
A herring	**Een haring**
	en hahring

Other essential expressions [*See also p. 56*]

Please can you ...	Kunt u ... alstublieft *koont oo ... uls-too-bleeft*
take the heads off?	de koppen afsnijden? *de koppen uf-sney-den*
clean them?	ze schoonmaken? *zer skone-mahken*
fillet them?	ze fileren? *zer fee-lairen*

Eating and drinking out

Ordering a drink

ESSENTIAL INFORMATION

- The place to ask for [*see p. 20*]
  EEN CAFÉ
- By law, the price list of drinks (TARIEF) must be displayed outside or in the window.
- There is waiter service in all cafés, but you can drink at the bar or counter if you wish.
- When the bill is presented, the amount will be inclusive of service and VAT (BTW). Tipping: some additional small change is often given.
- Cafés serve both non-alcoholic drinks and alcoholic drinks and are normally open all day. Cream/milk is always served separately when ordering coffee or tea.
- Children are allowed into bars

WHAT TO SAY

I'll have . . . please	**Ik wil graag . . . alstublieft**
	ik wil hrahk . . . uls-too-bl*eeft*
a cup of coffee	**een kop koffie**
	en kop koffee
a cup of tea	**een kop thee**
	en kop tay
with milk	**met melk**
	met melk
with lemon	**met citroen**
	met citr*oo*n
a glass of milk	**een glas melk**
	en hlus melk
a hot chocolate	**een kop chocolade**
	en kop shocol*ah*-der
a chilled chocolate	**een glas chocomel**
	en hlus shoco-m*el*
a mineral water	**een mineral water**
	en meener*ah*l w*a*h-ter
a lemonade	**een citroen limonade**
	en citr*oo*n leemo-nah-der
an orangeade	**een sinaasappel limonade**
	en s*ee*nahs-uppel leemo-n*a*h-der
a Coca-Cola	**een Coca-Cola**
	en coca-cola
a fresh orange juice	**een sinaasappelsap**
	en s*ee*nahs-uppel-sup
a blackcurrant drink	**een cassis**
	en c*u*ssis
an apple juice	**een appelsap**
	en *u*ppel-sup
a Pilsener beer (light ale)	**een Pils**
	en p*i*ls
a brown ale	**een donker bier**
	en donker b*ee*r
a bitter	**een bitter**
	en b*i*tter
a draught beer	**een bier van het vat**
	en beer vun et vut

A glass of . . .	Een glas . . .
	een hlus . . .
Two glasses of . . .	Twee glazen . . .
	tway hlahzen . . .
red wine	rode wijn
	roder weyn
white wine	witte wijn
	witter weyn
rosé	rosé
	roh-say
dry	droog
	drohk
sweet	zoet
	zoot
A bottle of . . .	Een fles . . .
	en fles . . .
sparkling wine	mousserende wijn
	moossay-render weyn
champagne	champagne
	shum-pun-yer
A whisky . . .	Een whiskey . . .
	en wiskee . . .
with ice	met ijs
	met eys
with water	met water
	met wah-ter
with soda	met sodawater
	met soda-wah-ter
A gin . . .	Een gin/ginever . . .
	en gin/yer-nayver . . .
and tonic	met tonic
	met ton-nik
with lemon	met citroen
	met citroon
A brandy/cognac	Een cognac
	en con-yuc

The following are local drinks you may like to try:

een oude klare   a pure, mature Dutch gin
en *owder* kl*ah*-rer
advocaat   a brandy and egg liqueur with
ut-voh-k*aht*   spices
bessenjenever   a red/blackcurrant gin liqueur
b*e*ssen-yer-n*ay*-ver
kersen brandewijn   cherry brandy
k*ai*rsen br*u*nder-weyn
citroen brandewijn   lemon brandy/gin (less sweet with
citr*oo*n br*u*nder-weyn   gin)
cognac grog   a hot diluted cognac with sugar
con-yuc hrok   and lemon slices
bisschop   a hot diluted red wine with orange
b*i*sskop   slices and spices

Other essential expressions:

Miss! [*This does not sound*   **Juffrouw!**
abrupt in Dutch]   yer-frow
Waiter!   **Ober!**
                                      ober

The bill, please   **De rekening, alstublieft**
                                      der r*ay*ker-ning uls-too-bl*ee*ft

How much does that come to?   **Hoeveel is dat samen?**
                                      h*oo*-vale is dut s*ah*-men

Is service included?   **Is het inclusief?**
                                      is et in-cloo-s*ee*f

Where is the toilet, please?   **Waar is het toilet?**
                                      wahr is et twah-l*e*t

Ordering a snack

ESSENTIAL INFORMATION

- Look for any of these places:
  SNELBUFFET (refreshment bar)
  CAFETARIA (low-priced snacks available; service not included)
  VISWINKEL
  GEBAKKEN VIS] ready fried fish available
- Apart from snacks, the cafetarias and snelbuffets also sell canned or bottled beer, tea and coffee.
- In some regions mobile vans do hot snacks.
- If you want a sandwich lunch, look out for KOFFIETAFEL. You will be served a variety of breads, cold meats, cheeses – possibly a hot dish – and a bowl of soup or a salad. Coffee, milk or tea are also usually included.
- For cakes, see p. 64; for ice-creams, see p. 66; for picnic-type snacks, see p. 70.

WHAT TO SAY

"ll have . . . please	Ik zou graag . . . hebben
	ik zow hrahk . . . hebben
a cheese roll	een broodje kaas
	en brote-yer kahs
a ham roll	een broodje ham
	en brote-yer hum
a hamburger	een hamburger
	en humbur-her
an omelet	een omelet
	en omerlet
with mushrooms	met champignons
	met shum-peen-yons
with ham	met ham
	met hum
with cheese	met kaas
	met kahs

These are some other snacks you might like to try:

een boterham	an open sandwich
en boter-rum	

een dubbele boterham en dub*ay*-lee bo*ter*-rum	a sandwich with two pieces of bread, i.e. like our sandwiches
een croquet en croh-ket	a croquette
een fricandel en free-cun-del	a minced meat roll
een saté en sateh	cubed meat (mostly pork or chicken on skewers with a spicy peanut sauce
een pannekoek en *pu*nner-kook	a pancake
een saucijze broodje en sow-s*eyzer*-brote-yer	a sausage roll
een broodje Tartaar en br*o*te-yer tar-t*a*r	a minced beef (raw) roll
een tosti en tostee	a toastie (ham and cheese)
een uitsmijter en *o*-eet-sm*ey*ter	two slices of bread with ham, roast beef or cheese, topped by two or three fried eggs
hutspot met klapstuk herts-pot met kl*u*p-sterk	carrots mashed with onions and potatoes, cooked with rib of pork
een kop erwtensoep en kop airten-soop	a cup of pea soup
een kop tomatensoep en kop toh-m*a*hten-soop	a cup of tomato soup
een kop groentesoep en kop hr*o*onter-soop	a cup of vegetable soup

You may wish to add to your order:

with chips	**met frites** met freet
with potato salad	**met aardappelsla** met *a*r-duppel-slah
with bread	**met brood** met br*o*te
with mustard	**met mosterd** met mostert
with ketchup	**met ketchup** met ket-shup
with mayonnaise	**met mayonaise** met mah-yon-*ai*ser

[*For other essential expressions, see 'Ordering a drink', p. 82*]

In a restaurant

ESSENTIAL INFORMATION

- The place to ask for: EEN RESTAURANT [*see p. 20*]
- You can eat at the following places:
  RESTAURANT
  HOTEL-RESTAURANT
  STATIONS-RESTAURATIE
  MOTEL
  CAFÉ-RESTAURANT
- By law, the menus must be displayed outside or in the window – and that is the *only* way to judge if a place is right for your needs.
- Self-service restaurants are not unknown, but most places have waiter service.
- A service charge is always added to the bill. Tipping is therefore optional.
- Most restaurants have children's portions.
- Some 700 restaurants offer a *tourist menu* (three courses) at a set price throughout the Netherlands although the courses themselves will differ from region to region. Restaurants participating in this scheme display the sign shown on the right.

- Hot meals are served from 12.00 p.m. – 2.00 p.m. at lunchtime and from 6.00 p.m. – 9.00/10.00 p.m. at night. After that many restaurants offer snacks for latecomers (soups, sausages, salads etc.). Many cities have Indonesian restaurants, where you will find the best *rijsttafel* (lit. 'rice table') outside Indonesia. This speciality consists of nine to ten varying dishes of meats, vegetables, fruits.

WHAT TO SAY

May I book a table?	Kan ik een tafel reserveren?
	kun ik en *tah*-fel ray-ser-*vairen*
I have booked a table	Ik heb een tafel gereserveerd
	ik hep en *tah*-fel he-ray-ser-*vairt*
A table ...	Een tafel ...
	en *tah*-fel ...
for one	voor één persoon
	vor ayn pair-*sohn*
for three	voor drie personen
	vor dree pair-*sohnen*
The à la carte menu, please	Het à la carte menu, alstublieft
	et ah la cart mer-*noo*
	uls-too-bl*ee*ft
The fixed-price menu	Het vastgestelde menu
	et v*ust*-her-stelder mer-n*oo*
Today's special menu	Het menu van de dag
	et mer-n*oo* vun der duk
The tourist menu	Het touristen menu
	et too-r*i*sten mer-n*oo*
What is this, please?	Wat is dit, alstublieft?
[*point to menu*]	wut is dit uls-too-bl*ee*ft
The wine list	De wijnlijst
	der weyn-leyst
A glass of wine	Een glas wijn
	en hlus weyn
A half-bottle	Een halve fles
	en h*u*lver fles
A bottle	Een fles
	en fles
A litre	Een liter
	en l*ee*ter
Red/white/rosé/house wine	Rode/witte/rosé/huis wijn
	roder/witter/roh-*say*/ho-ees weyn
Some more bread, please	Nog wat brood, alstublieft
	nok wut brote uls-too-bl*ee*ft
Some more wine	Nog wat wijn
	nok wut weyn
Some oil	Een beetje olie
	en b*ay*t-yer *o*lee
Some vinegar	Een beetje azijn
	en b*ay*t-yer ah-*zeyn*

Some salt	**Een beetje zout**
	en bayt-yer zowt
Some pepper	**Een beetje peper**
	en bayt-yer paper
Some water	**Een beetje water**
	en bayt-yer wah-ter
How much does that come to?	**Hoeveel is dat?**
	hoo-vale is dut
Is service included?	**Is het inclusief bediening?**
	is et in-cloo-seef ber-deening
Where is the toilet, please?	**Waar is het toilet?**
	wahr is et twah-let
Miss! [*This does not sound abrupt in Dutch*]	**Juffrouw!**
	yer-frow
Waiter!	**Ober!**
	ober
The bill, please	**De rekening, alstublieft**
	der rayker-ning uls-too-bleeft

Key words for courses, as seen on some menus

[*Ask this question if you want the waiter to remind you of the choice*]

What have you got in the way of . . .	**Wat voor . . . heeft u?**
	wut vor . . . hayft oo
STARTERS?	**VOORGERECHTEN**
	vor-her-rekten
SOUP?	**SOEP**
	soop
EGG DISHES?	**EIERGERECHTEN**
	ey-er-her-rekten
FISH?	**VIS**
	vis
MEAT?	**VLEES**
	vlays
GAME?	**WILD**
	wilt
FOWL?	**GEVOGELTE**
	her-voh-helter
VEGETABLES?	**GROENTE**
	hroonter
CHEESE?	**KAAS**
	kahs
FRUIT?	**FRUIT**
	fro-eet

ICE-CREAM?	IJS
DESSERT?	eys
	DESSERT
	des-sairt

UNDERSTANDING THE MENU

- You will find the names of the principal ingredients of most dishes on these pages:

Starters p. 70	Fruit p. 72
Meat p. 76	Cheese p. 71
Fish p. 79	Ice-cream p. 66
Vegetables p. 74	Dessert p. 64

Used together with the following lists of cooking and menu terms, they should help you decode the menu.

- These cooking and menu terms are for understanding – not for speaking.

Cooking and menu terms

aangemaakt	dressed
aspic	aspic
bouillon	broth, clear soup
doorgebakken	well-done
gebakken	fried, baked
gebraden	roasted
gefileerd	filleted
gegarneerd	garnished
geglazeerd	glazed
gegratineerd	au gratin
gegrilleerd	grilled
gekookt	boiled
gekruid	spiced
gelardeerd	larded
gemarineerd	marinated
gemengd	mixed
gepaneerd	dressed with eggs and breadcrumbs
gepocheerd	poached
geraapt	grated
gerookt	smoked
geroosterd	toasted
gesmoord	braised
gestoomd	steamed
gevulde	filled

gezouten	salted
in gelei	jellied
jus	gravy
kaasgerechten	cheese dishes
koude schotels	cold dishes
pikant	savoury
puree	mashed
ragout	ragout
rauw	raw
room	cream
salade/sla	salad
saté/sateh	meat cubes on sticks with peanut sauce
slagroom	whipped cream (with sugar)
soufflé	soufflé
wild en gevogelte	game and poultry
zoet	sweet
zuur	sour

Further words to help you understand the menu

aalbessen; rode, witte, zwarte	currants; red, white, black
aalbessen gelei	currant jelly
artisjok	artichoke
asperge	asparagus
aubergines	aubergines
augurken	pickled gherkins
avocado	avocado
bami	Indonesian noodle dish with diced pork and often shrimps
blinde vinken	veal fillet, filled with spiced minced veal, fried in butter
bloemkool	cauliflower
boerenkool (stamppot)	kale (hotchpotch)
borst	breast
bruine bonensoep	brown bean soup
brussels lof met ham en kaas	chicory with ham and cheese (oven dish)
chantilly crème met kastanje puree	whipped cream with chestnut purée
chinese kool	chinese cabbage
compote	stewed fruit
doperwten	peas
duitse biefstuk	hamburger steak

eend	duck
fazant	pheasant
flensjes	very thin pancakes
fondue	fondue
gebakken aardappels	fried potatoes
gebakken ananas	fried pineapple
gehakt	minced meat
gewelde boter	creamed butter
haantje	young cock
haas	hare
hachee	braised steak with onions, spices and vinegar
jachtschotel	hot-pot
kalfsvlees	veal
kappertjes saus	caper sauce
kapucijners	marrowfat peas
karbonade	chops
kervel	chervil
kip (gebraden)	chicken (roasted)
kotelet	cutlet
koude schotels	cold dishes
leverworst	liver sausage
loempia	Indonesian deep-fried pancake, filled with bamboo shoots, meat and vegetables
nasi goreng	Indonesian spicy rice dish
ossestaart soep	oxtail soup
paprika (gevulde)	green/red peppers (stuffed)
peterselie	parsley
prei	leeks
reebout	haunch of venison
roerei	scrambled egg
rolmop	rolled-up pickled herring filled with onion
russische eieren	hard boiled eggs with mayonnaise and caper sauce
schildpadsoep	turtle soup
snijbonen	green beans
sperciebonen	french beans
spruitjes	sprouts
taugé soup	bean sprouts soup
tonijn	tuna fish
zuurkool met spek	sauerkraut with boiled bacon

Health

ESSENTIAL INFORMATION

- For details of reciprocal health agreements between your country and the country you are visiting, visit your local Department of Health office at least one month before leaving, or ask your travel agent.
- In addition, it is preferable to purchase a medical insurance policy through the travel agent, a broker or a motoring organization.
- Take your own 'first line' first aid kit with you.
- For minor disorders and treatment at a drug store, see p. 42.
- For finding your own way to a doctor, dentist, drug store, or Health and Social Security Office (for reimbursement), see p. 20.
- The cost of the medical care of the tourist must be settled directly with the doctor, drug store, dentist, hospital, etc.
- Once in the Netherlands decide a definite plan of action in case of serious illness: communicate your problem to a near neighbour, the receptionist or someone you see regularly. You are then dependent on that person helping you obtain treatment.
- The name of the medical practitioner on duty at weekends and nights can be found in the local papers.

What's the matter?

I have a pain . . .	**Ik heb pijn . . . .**
	ik hep pain . . .
in my ankle	**aan mijn enkel**
	ahn mane *enkel*
in my arm	**aan mijn arm**
	ahn mane arm
in my back	**in mijn rug**
	in mane *rerk*
in my belly/tummy	**in mijn buik**
	in mane bo-eek
in my bowels	**in mijn ingewanden**
	in mane *in*-her-wunden
in my breast/chest	**in mijn borst**
	in mane borst

in my ear	**in mijn oor**
	in mane or
in my eyes	**in mijn oog**
	in mane *oak*
in my foot	**aan mijn voet**
	ahn mane voot
in my head	**in mijn hoofd**
	in mane hohft
in my heel	**aan mijn hiel**
	ahn mane heel
in my jaw	**aan mijn kaak**
	ahn mane kahk
in my leg	**in mijn been**
	in mane bane
in my neck	**in mijn hals**
	in mane huls
in my penis	**aan mijn penis**
	ahn mane *pay*-nis
in my shoulder	**in mijn schouder**
	in mane sk*owd*er
in my stomach/abdomen	**in mijn maag**
	in mane mahk
in my testicle	**in mijn testikel**
	in mane testee-kel
in my throat	**in mijn keel**
	in mane kale
in my vagina	**in mijn vagina**
	in mane vah-*hee*-nah
in my wrist	**aan mijn pols**
	ahn mane pols
I have a pain here *[point]*	**Ik heb hier pijn**
	ik hep here pain
I have toothache	**Ik heb kiespijn**
	ik hep k*ees*-pain
I have broken ...	**Ik heb ... gebroken**
	ik hep ... herbroken
my dentures	**mijn kunstgebit**
	mane koonst-her-bit
my glasses	**mijn bril**
	mane bril

I have lost . . .	Ik heb . . . verloren
	ik hep . . . ver-loren
my contact lenses	mijn contact lenzen
	mane con*tuct* lenzen
a filling	een vulling
	en verling
My child is ill	Mijn kind is ziek
	mane kint is zeek
He/she has a pain in his/her . . .	Hij/zij heeft pijn in zijn/haar . . .
	hey/zey hayft pain in zane/har . . .
ankle [*see list above*]	enkel
	enkel

How bad is it?

I'm ill	Ik ben ziek
	ik ben zeek
It is urgent	Het is dringend
	et is dring-ent
It's serious	Het is ernstig
	et is *airn*-stik
It's not serious	Het is niet ernstig
	et is neet *airn*-stik
It hurts	Het doet pijn
	et doot pain
It hurts a lot	Het doet erg pijn
	et doot airk pain
It doesn't hurt much	Het doet niet erg pijn
	et doot neet airk pain
The pain occurs . . .	De pijn komt . . .
	der pain komt . . .
every quarter of an hour	elk kwartier
	elk kwarteer
every half-hour	elk half uur
	elk hulf oor
every hour	elk uur
	elk oor
every day	elke dag
	elker duk

I have had it for . . .	**Ik heb het al . . .**
	ik hep et ul . . .
one hour/one day	**één uur/één dag**
	ayn oor/ayn duk
two hours/two days	**twee uur/twee dagen**
	tway oor/tway d*ah*-hen
It's a . . .	**Het is een . . .**
	et is en . . .
sharp pain	**scherpe pijn**
	sk*ai*rper pain
dull ache	**doffe pijn**
	d*o*ffer pain
nagging pain	**zeurende pijn**
	z*e*r-render pain
I feel . . .	**Ik voel me . . .**
	ik vool mer . . .
dizzy	**duizelig**
	d*o*-ee-zer-lik
sick	**misselijk**
	m*i*sser-lik
weak	**slap**
	slup
feverish	**koortsig**
	k*o*rtsik

Already under treatment for something else?

I take . . . regularly [*show*]	**Ik neem geregeld . . .**
	ik name her-r*ay*-helt . . .
this medicine	**dit medicijn**
	dit may-dee-s*ey*n
these pills	**deze pillen**
	d*a*zer p*i*llen
I have . . .	**Ik heb . . .**
	ik hep . . .
a heart condition	**een hart conditie**
	en hart con-d*ee*-tsee
haemorrhoids	**aambeien**
	*ah*m-bey-yen
rheumatism	**reumatiek**
	rer-mah-t*ee*k

I think I have ...	Ik geloof dat ik ... heb
	ik her-*lohf* dut ik ... hep
food poisoning	voedselvergiftiging
	vootsel-ver-*hif*tee-hing
sunstroke	een zonnesteak
	en zonner-stake
I'm ...	Ik lijd aan ...
	ik leyt ahn ...
diabetic	diabetes
	dee-ah-*bay*-tes
asthmatic	asthma
	ust-mah
I'm pregnant	Ik ben zwanger
	ik ben zw*ung*-er
I'm allergic to penicillin	Ik ben gevoelig voor penicilline
	ik ben her-*voolik* vor penicill*eener*

Other essential expressions

Please can you help?	Kunt u alstublieft helpen?
	koont oo uls-too-bl*eeft* helpen
A doctor, please	Een dokter, alstublieft
	en d*okter uls-too-bleeft
A dentist	Een tandarts
	en t*unt*-arts
I don't speak Dutch	Ik spreek geen nederlands
	ik sprake hayn *nay*-der-lunts
What time does ... arrive?	Hoe laat komt
	hoo laht komt ...
the doctor	de dokter?
	der d*okter
the dentist	de tandarts?
	der t*unt*-arts

From the doctor: key sentences to understand:

Take this . . .	Neem dit . . .
	name dit . . .
every day/hour	elke dag/uur
	*e*lker duk/oor
four times a day	vier maal per dag
	veer mahl pair duk
Stay in bed	Blijf in bed
	bleyf in bet
Don't travel . . .	Niet reizen . . .
	neet *re*yzen . . .
for . . . days/weeks	voor . . . dagen/weken
	vor . . . d*ah*-hen/w*a*ken
You must go to hospital	U moet naar het ziekenhuis
	oo moot nar et *ze*eken-h*o*-ees

Problems: complaints, loss, theft

ESSENTIAL INFORMATION

- Problems with:
  camping facilities, see p. 36
  household appliances, see p. 54
  health, see p. 94
  the car, see p. 110
- If the worst comes to the worst, find a police station.
  To ask the way, see p. 20.
- Look for:
  POLITIE
- If you lose your passport, report the loss to the nearest police station and go to your Consulate.

COMPLAINTS

I bought this . . .	**Ik kocht dit . . .**
	ik kokt dit . . .
today	**vandaag**
	vun-d*ah*k
yesterday	**gisteren**
	h*i*ster-ren
on Monday [*see p. 133*]	**maandag**
	m*ah*n-duk
It's no good	**Het is niet goed**
	et is neet hoot
Look	**Kijk**
	keyk
Here [*point*]	**Hier**
	here
Can you . . .	**Kunt u . . .**
	koont oo . . .
change it?	**het ruilen?**
	et r*o*-ee-len
mend it?	**het repareren?**
	et ray-pah-r*ay*-ren
Here's the receipt	**Hier is de bon**
	here is der bon
Can I have a refund?	**Mag ik terugbetaling?**
	muk ik ter-r*u*k-ber-tahling
Can I see the manager?	**Mag ik de chef spreken?**
	muk ik der shef sprayken

LOSS
[*See also 'Theft' below: the lists are interchangeable*]

I have lost . . .	**Ik heb . . . verloren**
	ik hep . . . verloren
my bag	**mijn tas**
	mane tus
my bracelet	**mijn armband**
	mane *a*rm-bunt
my camera	**mijn camera**
	mane c*ah*mer-rah
my car keys	**mijn autosleutels**
	mane *ow*to-slertels

I have lost . . .	Ik heb . . . verloren
	ik hep . . . verloren
my car logbook	mijn auto papieren
	mane *ow*to pah-*pee*-ren
my driving licence	mijn rijbewijs
	mane *rey*-ber-weys
my insurance certificate	mijn verzekeringsbewijs
	mane ver-*zay*kerrings-ber-weys
my jewellery	mijn juwelen
	mane yoo-*way*len
everything!	alles!
	ull-es

THEFT
[See also 'Loss' above: the lists are interchangeable]

Someone has stolen . . .	Iemand heeft . . . gestolen
	ee-munt hayft . . . her-stolen
my car	mijn auto
	mane *ow*-to
my car radio	mijn autoradio
	mane *ow*to-rahdio
my keys	mijn sleutels
	mane *sler*tels
my money	mijn geld
	mane helt
my necklace	mijn ketting
	mane *ket*ting
my passport	mijn paspoort
	mane *pus*port
my purse	mijn portemonnaie
	mane porter-mon*ay*
my radio	mijn radio
	mane *rah*dio
my tickets	mijn kaartjes
	mane *kart*-yers
my travellers' cheques	mijn reischeques
	mane *reys*-sheks
my wallet	mijn portefeuille
	mane porter-*foy*-yer
my watch	mijn horloge
	mane hor-*loh*-sher
my luggage	mijn bagage
	mane bah-*hah*-sher

LIKELY REACTIONS: key words to understand

Wait	**Wacht**
	wukt
When?	**Wanneer?**
	wun-nair
Where?	**Waar?**
	wahr
Name?	**Naam?**
	nahm
Address?	**Adres?**
	ah-dres
I can't help you	**Ik kan u niet helpen**
	ik kun oo neet helpen
Nothing to do with me	**Dat is mijn zaak niet**
	dut is mane zahk neet

The post office

ESSENTIAL INFORMATION

- To find a post office, see p. 20.
- Key words to look for:
  POSTKANTOOR
  POSTERIJEN
  POST EN SPAARBANK
- Look for the following sign:
- For stamps look for the word **POSTZEGELS** on a machine, or **ZEGELVERKOOP** or **FRANKEERZEGELS** at a post office counter.
- Stamps may be obtained at a stationery, provided postcards are also bought there.
- Stamp machines are yellow and red and contain the correct stamps for letters to EEC countries.
- Letter boxes are red and grey for twin boxes; others are red.
- For poste restante you should show your passport at the correct counter; a small fee is usually payable.

WHAT TO SAY

To England, please	**Naar Engeland, alstublieft** nar *eng*-er-lunt uls-too-bl*eeft*

[*Hand letters, cards or parcels over the counter*]

To Australia	**Naar Australië** nar ah-oostr*ah*-lee-yer
To the United States	**Naar de Verenigde Staten** nar der ver-*ay*-nik-der st*ah*-ten

[*For other countries, see p. 138*]

How much is . . .	**Hoeveel is . . .** h*oo*-vale is . . .
this parcel (to Canada)?	**dit pakje (naar Canada)?** dit p*u*k-yer (nar *ca*hnada)
a letter (to New Zealand)?	**een brief (naar Nieuw Zeeland)?** en breef (nar new-*zay*-lunt)
a postcard (to England)?	**een briefkaart (naar Engeland)?** en breef-kart (nar *eng*-er-lunt)
Airmail	**Luchtpost** l*er*kt-posst
Surface mail	**Zeepost** *zay*-posst
One stamp, please	**Eén postzegel, alstublieft** ayn p*os*-say-hel uls-too-bl*eeft*
Two stamps	**Twee postzegels** tway p*os*-say-hels
One (60) cent stamp	**Eén postzegel van (zestig) cent** ayn p*os*-say-hel vun (zestik) cent
I'd like to send a telegram	**Ik zou graag een telegram sturen** ik zow hrahk en telehr*u*m st*oo*-ren

Telephoning

ESSENTIAL INFORMATION

- Unless you read and speak Dutch well, it is best not to make phone calls by yourself. Go to a post office and write the town and number you want on a piece of paper. Add **persoonlijk gesprek** if you want a person-to-person call or **BO** if you want to reverse the charges.
- Public telephones, **TELEFOON**, are mainly glass with blue frames.
- Instructions on how to use the phone are printed inside in several languages.
- The code for the UK is 0944, and for the USA 091; then dial the number you want (less any initial 0).
- To ask the way to a public telephone or post office, see p. 20.

WHAT TO SAY

Where can I make a telephone call?	**Waar kan ik telefoneren?**
	wahr kun ik telefon*ay*-ren
Local/abroad	**Lokaal/buitenland**
	l*o*kahl/b*o*-ee-ten-lunt
I'd like this number . . .	**Ik wou dit nummer . . .**
[*show number*]	ik wow dit n*oo*mmer . . .
in England	**in Engeland**
	in eng-er-lunt
in Canada	**in Canada**
	in c*ah*nada
in the USA	**in de Verenigde Staten**
[*For other countries, see p. 138*]	in der ver-*ay*-nik-der st*ah*-ten
Can you dial it for me, please?	**Kunt u het voor me draaien, alstublieft?**
	koont oo et vor mer dr*ah*-yen uls-too-bl*ee*ft
How much is it?	**Hoeveel is het?**
	h*oo*-vale is et

Hello!	**Hallo!**
	hullo
May I speak to . . .?	**Mag ik met . . . spreken?**
	muk ik met . . . sprayken
Extension . . .	**Toestel . . .**
	too-stel . . .
I'm sorry, I don't speak Dutch	**Het spijt me, ik spreek geen Nederlands**
	et spate mer ik sprake hayn nay-der-lunts
Do you speak English?	**Spreekt u engels?**
	spraykt oo eng-els
Thank you, I'll phone back	**Dank u, ik bel terug**
	dunk oo ik bel ter-rerk
Good-bye	**Daag**
	dahk

LIKELY REACTIONS

That's (4.50 guilders)	**Dat is (vier gulden vijftig)**
	dut is (veer hoolden veyftik)
Cabin number (3)	**Cabine nummer (drie)**
	kah-beener noommer (dree)

[*For numbers, see p. 129*]

Don't hang up	**Niet ophangen**
	neet op-hung-en
I'm trying to connect you	**Ik probeer u te verbinden**
	ik probeer oo ter ver-bin-den
You're through	**U bent verbonden**
	oo bent ver-bonden
There's a delay	**Er is vertraging**
	er is ver-trah-hing
I'll try again	**Ik zal het nog eens proberen**
	ik zul et nok ayns probay-ren

Changing checks and money

ESSENTIAL INFORMATION

- Finding your way to a bank or change bureau, see p. 20.
- Look for these words or signs on buildings:
  BANK (bank)
  GRENSWISSELKANTOREN NV
  (more commonly given as **GWK**: these are to be found in stations and at the borders only)
  BUREAU DE CHANGE
- Banks are open weekdays 9:00 a.m. —4:00 p.m. The exchange offices **(WISSELKANTOREN)** are open Monday to Saturday and often in the evenings and on Sundays.
- To cash your own checks exactly as at home, use your credit card where you see the Eurocheque sign. Write in English.
- Have your passport ready.

WHAT TO SAY

I'd like to cash ...	Ik wou ... wisselen
	ik wow ... wisselen
this travellers' cheque	deze reischeque
	dazer rey.. hek
these travellers' cheques	deze reischeques
	dazer reys-sheks
this cheque	deze cheque
	dazer shek
I'd like to change this into guilders	Ik wou dit graag omwisselen in guldens
	ik wow dit hrahk om-wisselen in hooldens
Here's ...	Hier is ...
	here is ...
my banker's card	mijn cheque kaart
	mane shek kart
my passport	mijn paspoort
	mane pusport

For excursions into neighbouring countries

I'd like to change this . . .	**Ik wou dit graag omwisselen . . .**
[*show banknotes*]	ik wow dit hrahk *om*-wisselen . . .
into Belgian francs	**in belgische franken**
	in bel-hee-ser fr*u*nken
into French francs	**in franse franken**
	in fr*u*n-ser fr*u*nken
into German marks	**in duitse marken**
	in d*o*-eet-ser m*a*rken
What is the rate of exchange?	**Wat is de koers?**
	wut is der koors

LIKELY REACTIONS

Passport, please	**Paspoort, alstublieft**
	p*u*sport uls-too-bl*ee*ft
Sign here	**Hier tekenen**
	here t*a*ker-nen
Your banker's card, please	**Uw cheque kaart, alstublieft**
	oo sh*e*k k*a*rt uls-too-bl*ee*ft
Go to the cash desk	**Naar de kassa, alstublieft**
	n*a*r der k*u*ssa uls-too-bl*ee*ft

Car travel

ESSENTIAL INFORMATION

- Finding a filling station or garage, see p. 20.
  Is it a self-service station? Look out for: **ZELFBEDIENING**
  Grades of gasoline:
  NORMAAL (standard)
  SUPER (premium)
  DIESEL OLIE (diesel)
- 1 gallon is about 4½ litres (accurate enough for up to 6 gallons).
- The minimum sale is often 5 litres (less at self-service pumps)
- Filling stations may be able to deal with minor mechanical problems
  during the day only. For major repairs you have to go to a garage.
- All main roads are patrolled by the yellow cars of the Royal Dutch
  Touring Club (**ANWB**) between 7:00 a.m. and 12.00 p.m. Telephones
  have been installed along Holland's main roads to be used to obtain
  information from the local **ANWB** station. They will assist tourists
  whose cars break down. If you are not a member of an automobile
  club affiliated with the **AIT**, roadside service will be available if you
  become a temporary member of the **ANWB**.
- Unfamiliar road signs and warnings, see p. 125.

WHAT TO SAY
[*For numbers, see p. 129*]

(Nine) litres of . . .	**(Negen) liter . . .**
	(n*a*yhen) l*ee*ter . . .
(20) guilders of . . .	**Voor (twintig) gulden . . .**
	vor (tw*i*ntik) h*oo*lden . . .
Fill it up, please	**Vol alstublieft**
	vol uls-too-bl*eeft*
standard	**normaal**
	norm*ahl*
premium	**super**
	s*oo*per
diesel	**diesel**
	diesel

Will you check ...	Wilt u ... nakijken?
	wilt oo ... n*ah*-kayken
the oil?	de olie
	der *o*lee
the battery?	de accu
	der *u*ccoo
the radiator?	de radiator
	der rah-d*ee*-ah-tor
the tyres?	de banden
	der b*u*nden
I have run out of petrol	Ik zit zonder benzine
	ik zit zonder ben-*zee*ner
Can I borrow a can, please?	Kan ik een blik lenen, alstublieft?
	kun ik en blik *lay*-nen, uls-too-bleeft
My car has broken down	Ik heb auto-pech
	ik hep *owto*-pek
My car won't start	Mijn auto wil niet starten
	mane *owto* wil neet starten
I've had an accident	Ik heb een ongeluk gehad
	ik hep en *on*-her-luk her-h*ut*
I've lost my car keys	Ik heb mijn autosleutels verloren
	ik hep mane *owto*-slertels ver-loren
My car is ...	Mijn auto is ...
	mane *owto* is ...
two kilometres away	twee kilometer hier vandaan
	tway k*i*lo-may-ter here vun-d*ah*n
three kilometres away	drie kilometer hier vandaan
	dree k*i*lo-may-ter here vun-d*ah*n
Can you help me, please?	Kunt u me helpen, alstublieft?
	koont oo mer helpen uls-too-bleeft
Do you do repairs?	Doet u reparaties?
	doot oo ray-pah-*rah*tsees
I have a puncture	Ik heb een lekke band
	ik hep en *lekker* bunt
I have a broken windscreen	Ik heb een kapotte voorruit
	ik hep en kah-*potter* vor-ro-eet
I think the problem is here ... [point]	Ik denk dat het probleem hier is ...
	ik denk dut et pro-blame here is ...

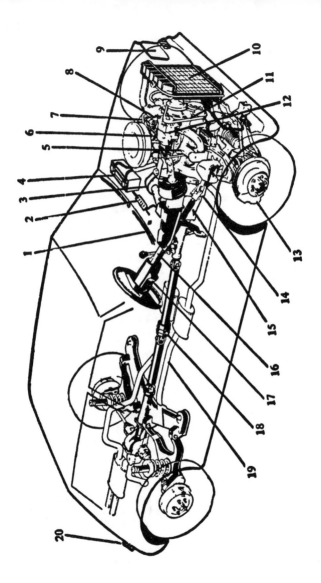

1	windscreen wipers	ruitenwissers	ro-ee-ten-wissers
2	fuses	zekeringen	zayker-ringen
3	heater	verwarming	ver-wahr-ming
4	battery	accu	uccoo
5	engine	motor	motor
6	fuel pump	benzinepomp	ben-zeener-pomp
7	starter motor	startmotor	start-mo-tor
8	carburettor	carburateur	car-boo-rah-ter
9	lights	lampen	lumpen
10	radiator	radiator	rah-dee-ah-tor
11	fan belt	ventilator-riem	ven-tee-lah-tor-reem
12	generator	dynamo	deena-mo
13	brakes	remmen	remmen
14	clutch	koppeling	kopper-ling
15	gear box	schakeldoos	skahkel-dose
16	steering	stuurinrichting	stoor-in-rikting
17	ignition	ontsteker	on-staker
18	transmission	transmissie	truns-mis-see
19	exhaust	uitlaat	o-eet-laht
20	indicators	richtingaanwijzers	rikting-ahn-weyzers

I don't know what is wrong	Ik weet niet wat het is
	ik wate neet wut et is
Can you ...	Kunt u ...
	koont oo ...
repair the fault?	de fout herstellen?
	der fowt *hair*-stellen
come and look?	eens kijken?
	ayns *kay*ken
estimate the cost?	de kosten schatten?
	der *kos*ten *sku*tten
write it down?	het opschrijven?
	et *op*-skrayven
Do you accept these coupons?	Accepteert u deze bonnen?
	uccep-*tairt* oo *da*zer bonnen
How long will the repairs take?	Hoelang duurt de reparatie?
	hoo-lung doort der ray-pah-*raht*see
When will the car be ready?	Wanneer is de auto klaar?
	*wun*nair is der *ow*to klar
Can I see the bill?	Mag ik de rekening zien?
	muk ik der *ra*ker-ning zeen
This is my insurance document	Dit is mijn verzekeringsbewijs
	dit is mane ver-*za*ker-rings-ber-*weys*

HIRING A CAR

Can I hire a car?	Kan ik een auto huren?
	kun ik en *ow*to *hoo*-ren
I need a car ...	Ik heb een auto nodig ...
	ik hep en *ow*to *no*dik ...
for two people	voor twee personen
	vor tway pair-*soh*nen
for five people	voor vijf personen
	vor veyf pair-*soh*nen
for one day	voor één dag
	vor ayn duk
for five days	voor vijf dagen
	vor veyf *dah*-hen
for a week	voor één week
	vor ayn wake

Can you write down . . .	**Kunt u opschrijven . . .**
	koont oo *op*-skray-ven . . .
the deposit to pay?	**de vooruit te betalen som?**
	der vor-*o*-eet ter ber-*tah*len som
the charge per kilometre?	**de prijs per kilometer?**
	der preys pair *ki*lo-may-ter
the daily charge?	**de prijs per dag?**
	der preys pair duk
the cost of insurance	**de verzekeringskosten?**
	der ver-*zaker*-rings-kos-ten
Can I leave it in (Edam)?	**Kan ik de auto in (Edam) achterlaten?**
	kun ik der *ow*to in (*ay*-dam) ukter-lah-ten
What documents do I need?	**Welke papieren heb ik nodig?**
	welker pah-*pee*-ren hep ik no*dik*

LIKELY REACTIONS

I don't do repairs	**Ik repareer niet**
	ik ray-pah-*rair* neet
Where is your car?	**Waar is uw auto?**
	wahr is oo *ow*to
What make is it?	**Welk merk is het?**
	welk mairk is et
Come back tomorrow/on Wednesday [*For days of the week, see p. 133*]	**Kom morgen/woensdag terug**
	kom mor-hen/*woons*-duk ter-rerk
We don't hire cars	**Wij verhuren geen auto's**
	way ver-*hooren* hayn *ow*tos
Your driving licence, please?	**Uw rijbewijs, alstublieft?**
	oo *rey*-ber-weys uls-too-bleeft
The mileage is unlimited	**Het kilometerverbruik is onbeperkt**
	et *ki*lomay-ter-ver-bro-eek is on-ber-*pairkt*

Public transport

ESSENTIAL INFORMATION

- Finding the way to the bus station, a bus, a trolley stop, the railway station and a taxi stand, see p. 20.
- Remember that lining up for buses is unheard of!
- It is less usual to hail a taxi in the street: go instead to a taxi stand or telephone a taxi service.
- These are the different types of trains, graded according to speed (fastest to slowest):
  TEE (Trans-Europa Express)
  INTERCITY NETWORK (national system of fast trains stopping only at a few stations)
  STOPTREINEN (stopping at all stations)
  Key words on signs: [see also p. 125]
  TREINKAARTJES (tickets)
  LOKET (ticket office)
  INGANG (entrance)
  UITGANG (exit)
  VERBODEN (forbidden)
  PERRON (platform)
  DOORGAAND VERKEER (transit passengers)
  WACHTKAMER (waiting room)
  INLICHTINGEN (information)
  BAGAGE DEPOT (left luggage)
  AANKOMST (arrivals)
  VERTREK (departures)
  NS (initials of Dutch railways)
  BUSHALTE (bus stop)
  DIENSTREGELING (timetable)
- Buying a ticket: train tickets are available at the station ticket office, in some main post offices and in some tobacconists'.
- When travelling by bus or trolley you usually pay as you enter. A bus and trolley STRIPPENKAART can be bought at post offices.
- There is a 'rover ticket' allowing unlimited travel through Holland for 3-7 days.
- A GROEP KAART permits unlimited travel by train for 2-6 persons for one day at a reduced rate.
- In some towns you can purchase a trolley ticket which allows you to interchange between trolleys in the one direction.

WHAT TO SAY

Where does the train for (Rotterdam) leave from?	**Van waar vertrekt de trein naar (Rotterdam)?** vun wahr ver-trekt der train nar (rotter-dum)
At what time does the train for (Rotterdam) leave?	**Hoe laat vertrekt de trein naar (Rotterdam)?** hoo laht ver-trekt der train nar (rotter-dum)
At what time does the train arrive in (Rotterdam)?	**Hoe laat komt de trein in (Rotterdam) aan?** hoo laht komt der train in (rotter-dum) ahn
Is this the train for (Rotterdam)?	**Is dit de trein naar (Rotterdam)?** is dit der train nar (rotter-dum)
Where does the bus for (Edam) leave from?	**Van waar vertrekt de bus naar (Edam)?** vun wahr ver-trekt der bus nar (ay-dum)
At what time does the bus leave for (Edam)?	**Hoe laat vertrekt de bus naar (Edam)?** hoo laat ver-trekt der bus nar (ay-dum)
At what time does the bus arrive at (Edam)?	**Hoe laat komt de bus in (Edam) aan?** hoo laht komt der bus in (ay-dum) ahn
Is this the bus for (Edam)?	**Is dit de bus naar (Edam)?** is dit der bus nar (ay-dum)
Do I have to change?	**Moet ik overstappen?** moot ik over-stuppen

Where does . . . leave from?	Van waar vertrekt . . .
	vun wahr ver-trekt . . .
the bus	de bus?
	der bus
the train	de trein?
	der train
the underground	de metro?
	der maytro
the boat/ferry	de boot/de veerboot?
	der boat/der vayr-boat
for the airport	naar het vliegveld?
	nar et vleek-velt
for the cathedral	naar de cathedraal?
	nar der kutter-drahl
for the beach	naar het strand?
	nar et strunt
for the market place	naar de markt?
	nar der markt
for the railway station	naar het spoorwegstation?
	nar et spor-wek-stat-see-on
for the town centre	naar het stadscentrum?
	nar et stuts-centrem
for the town hall	naar het gemeentehuis?
	nar et her-maynter-ho-ess
for the St Bavo church	naar de Sint Bavo kerk?
	nar der sint bahvoh kairk
for the swimming pool	naar het zwembad?
	nar et zwem-but
Is this . . .	Is dit . . .
	is dit . . .
the bus for the market place?	de bus voor het marktplein?
	der bus vor et markt-plain
the tram for the station?	de tram voor het spoowegstation?
	der trem vor et spor-wek-stat-see-on
Where can I get a taxi?	Waar kan ik een taxi krijgen?
	wahr kun ik en tuk-see kray-hen
Can you put me off at the right stop, please?	Kunt u mij op de juiste plaats afzetten, alstublieft?
	koont oo mey op der yo-ees-ter plahts uf-zetten uls-too-bleeft

Can I book a seat?	**Kan ik een plaats bespreken?**
	kun ik en plahts ber-sprayken
A single	**Een enkele**
	en enkerler
A return	**Een retour**
	en rer-toor
First class	**Eerste klas**
	airster klus
Second class	**Tweede klas**
	tway-der klus
One adult	**Eén volwassene**
	ayn vol-wusserner
Two adults	**Twee volwassenen**
	tway vol-wussernen
and one child	**en één kind**
	en ayn kint
and two children	**en twee kinderen**
	en tway kin-der-ren
How much is it?	**Hoeveel is het?**
	hoo-vale is et

LIKELY REACTIONS

Over there	**Daar**
	dar
Here	**Hier**
	here
Platform (1)	**(Eerste) perron**
	(airster) perron
At 16.00	**Om zestien ur**
[*For times, see p. 131*]	om zesteen oor
Change at (Dordrecht)	**In (Dordrecht) overstappen**
	in (dor-drekt) over-stuppen
Change at (the town hall)	**Bij het (Gemeentehuis) overstappen**
	bey et (her-maynter-ho-ees) over-stuppen
This is your stop	**Dit is uw halte**
	dit is oo hulter
There's only first class	**Er is alleen eerste klas**
	er is ul-layn aister klus
There's a supplement	**Er is toeslag op**
	er is too-sluk op

Leisure

ESSENTIAL INFORMATION

- Finding the way to a place of entertainment, see p. 20.
- For times of day, see p. 131.
- Important signs, see p. 125.
- At the seaside, beach chairs are for rent.
- No smoking in movies, theatres or concert halls, and in some restaurants.
- Movie houses always show films in the original language with Dutch subtitles.
- It is customary to leave one's coat in the cloakroom in theatres.

At what time does . . . open?	Hoe laat opent . . .
	hoo-laht opent . . .
the art gallery	de kunst galerij?
	der koonst hah-ler-rey
the botanical garden	de botanische tuin?
	der boh-tah-nee-ser to-een
the cinema	de bioscoop?
	der bee-os-cope
the concert hall	het concertgebouw?
	et con-sairt-her-ba-oo
the disco	de disco?
	der disco
the museum	het museum?
	et moo-sayem
the night club	de nacht club?
	der nukt cloop
the sports stadium	het stadion?
	et stah-dee-on
the swimming pool	het zwembad?
	et zwem-but
the theatre ·	het theater?
	et tay-ah-ter
the zoo	de dierentuin?
	der dee-ren-to-een

At what time does . . . close?	**Hoe laat sluit . . .**
	h*oo*-laht sl*o*-eet . . .
the skating rink	**de ijsbaan?**
[*see above list*]	der *eys*-bahn
At what time does . . . start?	**Hoe laat begint . . .**
	h*oo*-laht ber-h*i*nt . . .
the cabaret	**het cabaret?**
	et cah-bah-r*et*
the concert	**het concert?**
	et con-s*ai*rt
the film	**de film?**
	der film
the match	**de wedstrijd?**
	der wet-strait
the play	**het toneelstuk?**
	et toh-n*ay*l-sterk
the race	**de race?**
	der race
How much is it . . .	**Hoeveel is het . . .**
	h*oo*-vale is et . . .
for an adult?	**voor een volwassene?**
	vor *a*yn vol-w*u*sserner
for a child?	**voor een kind?**
	vor en kint
Two adults, please	**Twee volwassenen, alstublieft**
	tway vol-w*u*ssernen uls-too-bl*ee*ft
Three children, please	**Drie kinderen, alstublieft**
[*state price, if there is a choice*]	dree k*i*n-der-ren uls-too-bl*ee*ft
Stalls/circle	**Stalles/arena**
	st*u*l-les/ah-r*a*y-na
Do you have . . .	**Heeft u . . .**
	heyft oo . . .
a programme?	**een programma?**
	en proh-hr*u*mma
a guide book?	**een gids?**
	en hits
Where's the toilet, please?	**Waar is het toilet, alstublieft?**
	wahr is et twah-let uls-too-bl*ee*ft
Where's the cloakroom?	**Waar is de garderobe?**
	wahr is der harder-rober

I would like lessons in . . .	**Ik wou les hebben in . . .**
	ik wow les hebben in . . .
sailing	**zeilen**
	zaylen
skating	**schaatsen**
	skah-tsen
water skiing	**water skiën**
	wah-ter skee-yen
Can I hire . . .	**Kan ik . . . huren?**
	kun ik . . . hoo-ren
a boat?	**een boot**
	en boat
a fishing rod?	**een hengel**
	en heng-el
a deck chair?	**een dekstoel**
	en dek-stool
a parasol?	**een parasol**
	en pah-rah-sol
the necessary equipment?	**de benodigdheden**
	der ber-nodikt-hayden
How much is it . . .	**Hoeveel is het . . .**
	hoo-vale is et . . .
per day/per hour?	**per dag/per uur?**
	pair duk/pair oor
Do I need a licence?	**Heb ik een vergunning nodig?**
	hep ik en ver-hunning nodik

Asking if things are allowed

ESSENTIAL INFORMATION

- May one smoke here?
  May we smoke here?
  May I smoke here?
  Can one smoke here?
  Can we smoke here?
  Can I smoke here?

  Kan men hier roken?

- All these English variations can be expressed in one way in Dutch. To save space, only the first English version (May one . . .?) is shown below.

WHAT TO SAY

Excuse me, please . . .	**Neem me niet kwalijk . . .** name mer neet kwah-lek
May one . . .	**Kan men . . .** kun men . . .
camp here?	**hier kamperen?** here kum-pay-ren
come in?	**binnen komen?** binnen koh-men
dance here?	**hier dansen?** here dun-sen
fish here?	**hier vissen?** here vissen
get a drink here?	**hier wat te drinken krijgen** here wut ter drinken krey-hen
get out this way?	**hier door naar buiten gaan?** here dor nar bo-ee-ten hahn
leave one's things here?	**zijn spullen hier laten?** zane sperlen here lahten
look around?	**hier rondkijken?** here ront-kayken
park here?	**hier parkeren?** here par-kayren
picnic here?	**hier picknicken?** here picknicken

May one ...	**Kan men ...**
	kun men ...
sit here?	**hier zitten?**
	here *zi*tten
smoke here?	**hier roken?**
	here *ro*ken
swim here?	**hier zwemmen**
	here zwemmen
telephone here?	**hier telefoneren?**
	here telefon*ay*-ren
wait here?	**hier wachten?**
	here w*u*kten

LIKELY REACTIONS

Yes, certainly	**Ja, zeker**
	yah z*ay*ker
Help yourself	**Gaat uw gang**
	haht oo hung
I think so	**Ik geloof het wel**
	ik her-*loh*f et wel
Of course	**Natuurlijk**
	nah-*toor*-lik
Yes, but be careful	**Ja, maar wees voorzichtig**
	yah mar ways vor-*zi*ktik
No, certainly not	**Nee, beslist niet**
	nay ber-sl*i*st neet
I don't think so	**Ik geloof het niet**
	ik her-*loh*f et neet
Not normally	**Normaal niet**
	nor-m*ahl* neet
Sorry	**Sorry/Pardon**
	sorry/pur-d*o*n

Reference

PUBLIC NOTICES

● Key words on signs for drivers, pedestrians, travellers, shoppers and overnight guests.

AANKOMST	Arrival
ALLEEN BUSSEN	Buses only
BADKAMER	Bathroom
BAGAGE DEPOT	Left luggage
BAR	Bar
BELLEN	Ring (bell)
BEZET	Occupied
BRANDWEER	Fire brigade
BUFFET	Buffet
BUSHALTE	Bus stop
DAMES	Ladies
DOORGAAND VERKEER	Through traffic
DOUANE	Customs
DOUCHE	Shower
DRINKWATER	Drinking water
DUWEN	Push
EHBO	First aid
EENRICHTING VERKEER	One way traffic
EETKAMER	Dining room
EINDE SNELWEG	End of highway
FIETSERS OVERSTEKEN	Bicycles cross here
FIETSPAD	Bike path
GA	Go
GEEN INGANG	No entrance
GEEN TOEGANG	No admission
GERESERVEERD	Reserved
GESLOTEN	Closed
GEVAARLIJKE BOCHT	Dangerous curve
GIDS	Guide
HALT	Stop
HEET	Hot
HEREN	Gentlemen
INGANG	Entrance
INHALEN VERBODEN	Passing forbidden
INLICHTINGEN	Information/inquiries

KAMERS TE HUUR	Rooms vacant
KASSA	Cash desk
KLOPPEN	Knock (on door)
KOUD	Cold
KRUISWEG	Crossroads/junction
LANGZAAM RIJDEN	Drive slowly
LEVENSGEVAARLIJK	Danger
LICHTEN AAN	Lights on
LIFT	Lift/elevator
METRO	Underground (railway/train)
NIET AANRAKEN	Do not touch
NIET BADEN/ZWEMMEN	No bathing/swimming
NIET PARKEREN	No parking
NIET ROKEN	No smoking
NOODUITGANG	Emergency exit
ONBEWAAKTE OVERWEG	Unguarded level crossing
ONGELUK	Accident
OPEN	Open
OPGELET (TREINEN)	Beware (trains)
OVERSTEKEN	Cross over
OVERTREDERS WORDEN GESTRAFT	Trespassers will be prosecuted
OVERWEG	Level crossing
PARKEERPLAATS	Parking place
PARKEERSCHIJF VERPLICHT	Parking tokens obligatory
PARKEREN BEPERKT	Limited parking
PAS OP VOOR DE HOND	Beware of the dog
PERRON	Platform
PLAATSBEWIJZEN	Tickets
POLITIE	Police
PORTIER	Porter
PRIVÉ	Private
RECEPTIE	Reception
RECHTS HOUDEN	Keep right
RECHTS VOORRANG	Priority to the right
RESERVERINGEN	Reservations
RESTAURATIEWAGEN	Dining car
ROKEN TOEGESTAAN	Smoking permitted
ROLTRAP	Escalator
SCHOOL	School
SLAAPWAGEN	Sleeping car

SLECHT WEGDEK	Bad road surface
SLIP GEVAAR	Slippery road
SNELWEG	Highway
SOUTERRAIN	Basement
SPECIALE AANBIEDING	Special offer
SPREEKUUR	Doctor's office hours
STAANPLAATSEN	Standing room
STEENSLAG	Loose chippings
STOP	Stop
TE HUUR	For rent
TE KOOP	For sale
TOL	Toll
TREKKEN	Pull
TWEE-RICHTING VERKEER	Two-way traffic
UIT	Out
UITGANG	Exit
UITVERKOOP	Sale
VERBODEN	Forbidden/prohibited
VERDIEPING: EERSTE/ TWEEDE/DERDE	Floor: first/ second/third
VERKEERSLICHTEN	Traffic lights
VERTREK	Departure
VIADUCT	Viaduct
VOETGANGERS	Pedestrians
VOOR ZWAAR VERKEER	For heavy traffic
VOORRANG VERLENEN	Yield
VOORRANGSWEG	Major road
VOORSORTEREN	Filter/get in lane
VRIJ	Vacant
VRIJE TOEGANG	Free entrance
WAARSCHUWING	Warning
WACHT!	Wait!
WACHTKAMER	Waiting room
WEG VERSMALLING	Road narrowing
WEGOMLEGGING	Detour
WERK IN UITVOERING	Construction ahead
ZACHTE BERM	Soft shoulder
ZIEKENHUIS	Hospital

ABBREVIATIONS

ANWB	Algemene Nederlandse Wielrijders Bond	Royal Dutch Touring Club
aub	alstublieft	if you please
BTW	Bijzonder Toegevoegde Waarde	VAT
CS	Centraal Station	Central Station
cm	centimeter	centimetre
Dr	Doctor	doctor
enz	enzovoort	et cetera
Expo	Expositie	exposition
F/Fl	gulden	guilder
GWK	Grens Wisselkantoor	border exchange office
Hr	Heer	Mr
KLM	Koninklijke Nederlandse Luchtvaartmaatschappij	Royal Dutch Airlines
km	kilometer	kilometre
KNAC	Koninklijke Nederlandse Automobiel Club	Royal Dutch Automobile Association
kw	kilowatt	kilowatt
Mej	Mejuffrouw	Miss
m	meter	metre
M	Metro	underground train
Mevr Mw	Mevrouw	Mrs
med	medisch	medical
Ned/Nld	Nederland	the Netherlands
NS	Nederlandse Spoorwegen	Dutch Railways
NFN	Nederlandse Federatie van Naturalisme	Netherlands Federation of Naturalism
NJHC	Nederlandse Jeugdherberg Centrale	Dutch Youth Hostel Organization
NNTB	Nederlands Nationaal Touristen Bureau	Netherlands National Tourist Office
NRC	Nederlands Reserveer Centrum	Netherlands (National) Reservation
Pol	Politie	police
Prov	Provincie	province
PTT	Post Telegraaf Telefoon	the Post Office
TV	Televisie	television
VVV	Vereniging Vreemdelingen Verkeer	tourist office
WW	Wegenwacht	Automobile Association
Z	Zelfbediening	Self-service
s	zuid	south

NUMBERS
Cardinal numbers

0	nul	nerl
1	één	ayn
2	twee	tway
3	drie	dree
4	vier	veer
5	vijf	veyf
6	zes	zes
7	zeven	zayven
8	acht	ukt
9	negen	nayhen
10	tien	teen
11	elf	elf
12	twaalf	twahlf
13	dertien	dairteen
14	veertien	vairteen
15	vijftien	veyfteen
16	zestien	zesteen
17	zeventien	zayventeen
18	achttien	ukteen
19	negentien	nayhenteen
20	twintig	twintik
21	éénentwintig	ayn-en-twintik
22	tweeëntwintig	tway-en-twintik
23	drieëntwintig	dree-en-twintik
24	vierentwintig	veer-en-twintik
25	vijfentwintig	veyf-en-twintik
26	zesentwintig	zes-en-twintik
27	zevenentwintig	zayven-en-twintik
28	achtentwintig	ukt-en-twintik
29	negenentwintig	nayhen-en-twintik
30	dertig	dairtik
31	éénendertig	ayn-en-dairtik
35	vijfendertig	veyf-en-dairtik
40	veertig	vairtik
41	éénenveertig	ayn-en-vairtik
50	vijftig	veyftik
51	éénenvijftig	ayn-en-veyftik
60	zestig	zestik
70	zeventig	zayventik
80	tachtig	tuktik
81	éénentachtig	ayn-én-tuktik

90	negentig	nayhentik
95	vijfennegentig	veyf-en-nayhentik
100	honderd	hondert
101	honderdéén	hondert-ayn
102	honderdtwee	hondert-tway
125	hondervijfentwintig	hondert-veyf-en-twintik
150	honderdvijftig	hondert-veyftik
175	hondervijfenzeventig	hondert-veyf-en-zayventik
200	tweehonderd	tway-hondert
300	driehonderd	dree-hondert
400	vierhonderd	veer-hondert
500	vijfhonderd	veyf-hondert
1000	duizend	do-ee-zent
1100	elfhonderd	elf-hondert
3000	drieduizend	dree-do-ee-zent
5000	vijfduizend	veyf-do-ee-zent
10,000	tienduizend	teen-do-ee-zent
100,000	honderdduizend	hondert-do-ee-zent
1,000,000	één miljoen	ayn mil-yoon

Ordinal numbers

1st.	eerste	air-ster
2nd	tweede	tway-der
3rd	derde	dair-der
4th	vierde	veer-der
5th	vijfde	veyf-der
6th	zesde	zes-der
7th	zevende	zayven-der
8th	achtste	ukt-ster
9th	negende	nayhen-der
10th	tiende	teender
11th	elfde	elf-der
12th	twaalfde	twahlf-der

TIME

What time is it?	Hoe laat is het?
	hoo laht is et
It's ...	Het is ...
	et is ...
one o'clock	één uur
	ayn oor

two o'clock	twee uur
	tway oor
three o'clock	drie uhr
	dree oor
four o'clock	vier uur
	veer oor
in the morning	's morgens
	smor-hens
in the afternoon	's middags
	smid-ducks
in the evening	's avonds
	sahvents
at night	's nachts
	snukts
It's ...	Het is ...
	et is ...
noon	middag
	mid-duk
midnight	middernacht
	midder-nukt
It's ...	Het is ...
	et is ...
five past five	vijf over vijf
	veyf over veyf
ten past five	tien over vijf
	teen over veyf
a quarter past five	kwart over vijf
	kwart over veyf
twenty past five	twintig over vijf
	twintik over veyf
twenty-five past five	vijf vóór half zes
	veyf vor hulf zes
half past five	half zes
	hulf zes
twenty-five to six	vijf over half zes
	veyf over hulf zes
twenty to six	twintig vóór zes
	twintik voor zes
a quarter to six	kwart vóór zes
	kwart vor zes
ten to six	tien vóór zes
	teen vor zes
five to six	vijf vóór zes
	veyf vor zes

At what time . . . (does the train leave)?	Hoe laat . . . (vertrekt de trein)? hoo laht . . . (ver-trekt der train)
At . . .	Om . . . om . . .
13.00	dertien uur dair-teen oor
14.05	veertien uur vijf vairteen uur veyf
15.10	vijftien uur tien veyfteen oor teen
16.15	zestien uur vijftien zesteen oor veyfteen
17.20	zeventien uur twintig zayventeen oor twintik
18.25	achttien uur vijfentwintig ukteen oor veyf-en-twintik
19.30	negentien uur dertig nayhenteen oor dairtik
20.35	twintig uur vijfendertig twintik oor veyf-en-dairtik
21.40	éénentwintig uur veertig ayn-en-twintik oor veertik
22.45	tweeëntwintig uur vijfenveertig tway-en-twin-tik oor veyf-en-vairtik
23.50	drieëntwintig uur vijftig dree-en-twintik oor veyftik
0.55	vijf minuten vóór één veyf mee-nooten vor ayn
in ten minutes	binnen tien minuten binnen teen mee-nooten
In a quarter of an hour	binnen een kwartier binnen en kwar-teer
in half an hour	binnen een half uur binnen en hulf oor
in three-quarters of an hour	binnen drie kwartier binnen dree kwar-teer

DAYS

Monday	**maandag**
	m*ah*n-du*k*
Tuesday	**dinsdag**
	d*i*ns-du*k*
Wednesday	**woensdag**
	w*oo*ns-du*k*
Thursday	**donderdag**
	d*o*nder-du*k*
Friday	**vrijdag**
	vr*ey*-du*k*
Saturday	**zaterdag**
	z*ah*ter-du*k*
Sunday	**zondag**
	z*o*n-du*k*
last Monday	**verleden maandag**
	ver-*lay*den m*ah*n-du*k*
next Tuesday	**aánstaande dinsdag**
	*ah*n-stahn-der d*i*ns-du*k*
on Wednesday	**op woensdag**
	op w*oo*ns-du*k*
on Thursdays	**op donderdag**
	op d*o*nder-du*k*
until Friday	**tot vrijdag**
	tot vr*ey*-du*k*
before Saturday	**vóór zaterdag**
	vor z*ah*ter-du*k*
after Sunday	**na zondag**
	na z*o*n-du*k*
the day before yesterday	**eergisteren**
	air-histeren
two days ago	**twee dagen geleden**
	tway d*ah*-hen her-*laden*
yesterday	**gisteren**
	h*i*steren
yesterday morning	**gisterenmorgen**
	h*i*steren-mor-hen
yesterday afternoon	**gisterenmiddag**
	h*i*steren-m*i*d-duk
last night	**gisterenavond**
	h*i*steren-*ah*vent
today	**vandaag**
	v*u*n-d*ah*k

this morning	**vanmorgen** vun-mor-hen
this afternoon	**vanmiddag** vun-mid-duk
tonight	**vanavond** vun-*ah*vent
tomorrow	**morgen** mor-hen
tomorrow morning	**morgenochtend** mor-hen-oktent
tomorrow afternoon	**morgenmiddag** mor-hen-mid-duk
tomorrow evening	**morgenavond** mor-hen-ahvent
the day after tomorrow	**overmorgen** over-mor-hen

MONTHS AND DATES

January	Januari
	yun-oo-*ah*-ree
February	februari
	fay-broo-*ah*-ree
March	maart
	mart
April	april
	ah-pr*i*l
May	mei
	may
June	juni
	yoo-nee
July	juli
	yoo-lee
August	augustus
	ow-hers-tes
September	september
	september
October	oktober
	okt*o*ber
November	november
	nov*e*mber
December	december
	day-sember
in January	in januari
	in yun-oo-*ah*-ree
until February	tot februari
	tot fay-broo-*ah*-ree
before March	vóór maart
	vor mart
after April	na april
	na ah-pr*i*l
during May	gedurende mei
	her-*doo*-render may
not until June	niet tot juni
	neet tot yoo-nee
the beginning of July	begin juli
	ber-h*i*n yoo-lee
middle of August	midden augustus
	m*i*dden ow-hers-tes

end of September	eind September
	*e*ynt september
last month	verleden maand
	ver-*la*den mahnt
this month	deze maand
	d*a*zer mahnt
next month	volgende maand
	*vo*l-hender mahnt
in spring	in de lente
	in der *le*nter
in summer	in de zomer
	in der *zo*mer
in autumn	in de herfst
	in der hairfst
in winter	in de winter
	in der *wi*nter
this year	dit jaar
	dit yar
last year	verleden jaar
	ver-*la*den yar
next year	volgend jaar
	*vo*l-hent yar
in 1982	in negentien (honderd) tween•tachtig
	in *na*yhenteen (hondert) tway-en•t*u*ktik
in 1985	in negentien (honderd) vijfen•tachtig
	in *na*yhenteen (hondert) v*e*yf-en•t*u*ktik
in 1990	in negentien (honderd) negentig
	in *na*yhenteen (hondert) *na*yhentik
What is the date today?	Wat is de datum vandaag?
	wut is der d*a*h-tum vun-d*a*hk
It's the 6th of March	Het is zes maart
	et is zes mart
It's the 12th of April	Het is twaalf april
	et is twahlf ah-pr*i*l
It's the 21st of August	Het is éénentwintig augustus
	et is *a*yn-en-tintik ow-*he*rs-tes

Public holidays

● Shops, schools and offices are closed on the following dates:

1 January	Nieuwjaarsdag	New Year's Day
...	Paasmaandag	Easter Monday
	Pinkstermaandag	Whitsun Monday
	Hemelvaartsdag	Ascension Day
30 April	Koninginnedag	The Queen's birthday
25 December	Eerste Kerstdag	Christmas Day
26 December	Tweede Kerstdag	Boxing Day
5 May	Bevrijdingsdag	Liberation Day
		(once every 5 years)

COUNTRIES AND NATIONALITIES
Countries

America	**Amerika** ah-may-ree-kah
Australia	**Australië** ah-oo-strah-lee-yer
Austria	**Oostenrijk** oh-sten-reyk
Belgium	**België** bel-hee-yer
Britain	**Groot Britannië** hrote brit-tun-yer
Canada	**Canada** cahnada
Czech Republic	**Tsjechië** che-kee-yer
East Africa	**Oost Afrika** ohst-ah-free-kah
Eire	**Ierland** eer-lunt
England	**Engeland** eng-er-lunt
France	**Frankrijk** frunk-reyk
Germany	**Duitsland** do-eets-lunt
Greece	**Griekenland** hree-ken-lunt
India	**India** indee-yah
Indonesia	**Indonesië** indo-nay-see-yer
Italy	**Italië** ee-tah-lee-yer
Luxembourg	**Luxemburg** looksem-burk
The Netherlands	**Nederland** nay-der-lunt
New Zealand	**Nieuw Zeeland** neew zay-lunt

Pakistan	**Pakistan**
	pah-kee-st*u*n
Poland	**Polen**
	poh-len
Portugal	**Portugal**
	por-too-hul
Scotland	**Schotland**
	sk*o*t-lunt
South Africa	**Zuid Afrika**
	z*o*-eet *a*h-free-kah
Spain	**Spanje**
	sp*u*n-yer
Surinam	**Suriname**
	soo-ree-n*a*h-mer
Switzerland	**Zwitserland**
	zw*i*tser-lunt
Wales	**Wales**
	wayls
West Indies	**West Indië**
	west *i*ndee-yer
Yugoslavia	**Joego-Slavië**
	yoo-hoh-sl*a*h-vee-yer

Nationalities
[Use the first alternative for men, the second for women]

American	amerikaan/amerikaanse
	ah-may-ree-kahn/ah-may-ree-kahn-ser
Australian	australiër/australische
	ah-oo-strah-lee-yer/ah-oo-strah-lee-ser
British	brit/britse
	brit/britser
Canadian	canadees/canadese
	cahna-days/cahna-dayser
East African	oost afrikaner/oost afrikaanse
	ohst-ah-free-kahner/ohst ah-free-kahn-ser
English	engelsman/engelse
	eng-els-mun/eng-el-ser
Indian	indiër/indische
	indee-yer/indee-ser
Irish	ier/ierse
	eer/eer-ser
New Zealander	nieuw zeelander/nieuw zeelandse
	neew-zay-lun-der/neew-zay-lunt-ser
Pakistani	pakistaner/pakistaanse
	puk-kee-stah-ner/puk-kee-stahn-ser
Scots	schot/schotse
	skot/skotser
South African	zuid afrikaner/zuid afrikanse
	zo-eet ah-free-kahner/zo-eet ah-free-kahn-ser
Welsh	welliser
	wellee-ser
West Indian	west indiër/west indische
	west indee-yer/west indee-ser

DEPARTMENT STORE GUIDE

Aardewerk	Earthenware
Baby uitzet	Layette
Bedden	Beds
Beneden verdieping	Ground floor
Blouses	Blouses
Boeken	Books
Camping	Camping
Cadeaux	Gifts
Ceintuurs	Belts
Corsetten	Girdles
Dames modes	Ladies' fashions
Dassen	Ties
Dekens	Blankets
Derde verdieping	Third floor
Diepvries	Frozen food
Doe-het-zelf afdeling	DIY department
Eerste verdieping	First floor
Electriciteits-benodigdheden	Electrical appliances
Etenswaren	Food
Fietsen	Bicycles
Fotografie	Photography
Fournituren	Haberdashery
Fruit	Fruit
Geschenken	Gifts
Glaswerk	Glassware
Gordijnen	Curtains
Grammofoonplaten	Records
Handschoenen	Gloves
Handwerken	Needlework
Heren confectie/modes	Men's fashions
Ijzerwaren	Hardware
Inlichtingen	Information/inquiries
Juwelen	Jewellery
Keuken inrichting	Kitchen furniture
Kinderkleding	Children's clothes
Knippatronen	Paper patterns
Kousen	Hosiery
Kussens	Cushions/pillows
Lederwaren	Leather goods
Linnen	Linen
Lingerie	Lingerie

Meubels	Furniture
Overhemden	Shirts
Panties	Tights
Parfumerieën	Perfumery
Parterre	Ground floor
Porcelein	China
Pullovers	Pullovers
Radio	Radio
Reisartikelen	Travel goods
Riemen	Belts
Schrijfbeno ligdheden	Stationery
Schoenen	Shoes
Schoonheidsmiddelen	Cosmetics
Schoonmaakartikelen	Cleaning materials
Souterrain	Basement
Speelgoed	Toys
Sportartikelen	Sports goods
Stofferingen	Draperies
Tabaksarti;elen	Tobacco
Tapijten	Carpets
Televisie	Television
Tweede verdieping	Second floor
Vierde verdieping	Fourth floor
Wol	Woollens

CONVERSION TABLES

Read the centre column of these tables from right to left to convert from metric to imperial and from left to right to convert from imperial to metric e.g. 5 litres = 8.80 pints; 5 pints = 2.84 litres.

pints		litres		gallons		litres
1.76	1	0.57		0.22	1	4.55
3.52	2	1.14		0.44	2	9.09
5.28	3	1.70		0.66	3	13.64
7.07	4	2.27		0.88	4	18.18
8.80	5	2.84		1.00	5	22.73
10.56	6	3.41		1.32	6	27.28
12.32	7	3.98		1.54	7	31.82
14.08	8	4.55		1.76	8	36.37
15.84	9	5.11		1.98	9	40.91

ounces		grams		pounds		kilos
0.04	1	28.35		2.20	1	0.45
0.07	2	56.70		4.41	2	0.91
0.11	3	85.05		6.61	3	1.36
0.14	4	113.40		8.82	4	1.81
0.18	5	141.75		11.02	5	2.27
0.21	6	170.10		13.23	6	2.72
0.25	7	198.45		15.43	7	3.18
0.28	8	226.80		17.64	8	3.63
0.32	9	225.15		19.84	9	4.08

inches		centimetres		yards		metres
0.39	1	2.54		1.09	1	0.91
0.79	2	5.08		2.19	2	1.83
1.18	3	7.62		3.28	3	2.74
1.58	4	10.16		4.37	4	3.66
1.97	5	12.70		5.47	5	4.57
2.36	6	15.24		6.56	6	5.49
2.76	7	17.78		7.66	7	6.40
3.15	8	20.32		8.65	8	7.32
3.54	9	22.86		9.84	9	8.23

miles		kilometres
0.62	1	1.61
1.24	2	3.22
1.86	3	4.83
2.49	4	6.44
3.11	5	8.05
3.73	6	9.66
4.35	7	11.27
4.97	8	12.87
5.59	9	14.48

A quick way to convert kilometres to miles: divide by 8 and multiply by 5. To convert miles to kilometres: divide by 5 and multiply by 8.

fahrenheit (°F)	centigrade (°C)		lbs/ sq in	k/ sq cm
212°	100° boiling point		18	1.3
100°	38°		20	1.4
94.8°	36.9° body temperature		22	1.5
86°	30°		25	1.7
77°	25°		29	2.0
68°	20°		32	2.3
59°	15°		35	2.5
50°	10°		36	2.5
41°	5°		39	2.7
32°	0° freezing point		40	2.8
14°	−10°		43	3.0
−4°	−20°		45	3.2
			46	3.2
			50	3.5
			60	4.2

To convert °C to °F: divide by 5, multiply by 9 and add 32. To convert °F to °C: take away 32, divide by 9 and multiply by 5.

CLOTHING SIZES

Remember – always try on clothes before buying. Clothing sizes are usually unreliable.

women's dresses and suits

Europe	38	40	42	44	46	48
UK	32	34	36	38	40	42
USA	10	12	14	16	18	20

men's suits and coats

Europe	46	48	50	52	54	56
UK and USA	36	38	40	42	44	46

men's shirts

Europe	36	37	38	39	41	42	43
UK and USA	14	14½	15	15½	16	16½	17

socks

Europe	38–39	39–40	40–41	41–42	42–43
UK and USA	9½	10	10½	11	11½

shoes

Europe	34	35½	36½	38	39	41	42	43	44	45
UK	2	3	4	5	6	7	8	9	10	11
USA	3½	4½	5½	6½	7½	8½	9½	10½	11½	12½

Do it yourself

Some notes on the language

This section does not deal with 'grammar' as such. The purpose here is to explain some of the most obvious and elementary nuts and bolts of the language, based on the principal phrases included in the book. This information should enable you to produce numerous sentences of your own making, although you will obviously still be fairly limited in what you can say.

There is no pronunciation guide in this section, partly because it would get in the way of the explanations and partly because you have to do it yourself at this stage if you are serious – work out the pronunciation from all the earlier examples.

THE

All nouns in Dutch belong to one of two genders: common (originally masculine or feminine) or neuter, irrespective of whether they refer to living beings or inanimate objects.

the	common	neuter	plural
the address		het adres	de adressen/the addresses
the apple	de appel		de appels/the apples
the bill	de rekening		de rekeningen/the bills
the cup of tea	de kop thee		de koppen thee/the cups of tea
the glass of beer		het glas bier	de glazen bier/the glasses of beer
the key	de sleutel		de sleutels/the keys
the luggage	de bagage		
the menu		het menu	de menu's/the menus
the newspaper	de krant		de kranten/the newspapers
the sandwich	de dubbele boterham		de dubbele boterhammen/the sandwiches
the suitcase	de koffer		de koffers/the suitcases
the telephone directory		het telefoon boek	de telefoon boeken/the telephone directories
the timetable	de dienstregeling		de dienstregelingen/the timetables

Important things to remember

- *The* is **de** before a common noun, and **het** before a neuter singular noun.
- There is no way of telling if a noun is common or neuter. You have to learn and remember its gender. Obviously if you are reading a word with **de** or **het** in front of it you can tell its gender immediately: **de appel** is common (*c.* in dictionaries) and **het menu** is neuter (*n.* in dictionaries).
- Does it matter? Not unless you want to make a serious attempt to speak correctly and scratch beneath the surface of the language. You would be understood if you said **de menu** or or even **het appel**, providing your pronunciation was good.
- There is one exception however: all diminutives are neuter; they end in **-je**, **-tje** or **-pje**.
- *The* is always **de** before a noun in the plural.
- As a general rule, a noun adds an 's' or 'en' to become plural. But watch out for the many exceptions such as **kind/kinderen**, **menu/menu's**.
- In Dutch, as in English, luggage has no plural.

Practise saying and writing these sentences in Dutch:

Have you got the key?	**Heeft u de sleutel?**
Have you got the luggage?	**Heeft u ... ?**
Have you got the telephone directory?	
Have you got the menu?	
I'd like the key	**Ik zou graag de sleutel hebben**
I'd like the luggage	**Ik zou graag ...**
I'd like the bill	
I'd like the keys	
Where is the key?	**Waar is de sleutel?**
Where is the timetable?	**Waar is ... ?**
Where is the address?	
Where is the suitcase?	
Where are the keys?	**Waar zijn sleutels?**
Where are the sandwiches?	**Waar zijn ... ?**
Where are the apples?	
Where are the suitcases?	
Where is the luggage?	**Waar is ... ?**
Where can I get the key?	**Waar kan ik de sleutel krijgen?**
Where can I get the address?	**Waar kan ik ... krijgen?**
Where can I get the timetables?	

Now make up more sentences along the same lines. Try adding *please*: alstublieft, at the end.

A/AN

a/an	singular	plural	some/any
an address	een adres	addressen	addresses
an apple	een appel	appels	apples
a bill	een rekening	rekeningen	bills
a cup of tea	een kop thee	koppen thee	cups of tea
a glass of beer	een glas bier	glazen bier	glasses of beer
a key	een sleutel	sleutels	keys
...	de bagage	...	luggage
a menu	een menu	menu's	menus
a newspaper	een krant	kranten	newspapers
a sandwich	een dubbele boterham	dubbele botterhammen	sandwiches
a suitcase	een koffer	koffers	suitcases
a telephone directory	een telefoon boek	telefoon boeken	telephone directories
a timetable	een dienstregeling	dienstregelingen	timetables

Important things to remember

- *A* or *an* is always **een** before a noun, whether common or neuter.
- *Some* or *any* before a noun in the plural has no equivalent in Dutch. Just leave it out. Examples of this can be seen in the phrases marked* below.

Practise saying and writing these sentences in Dutch:

Have you got a bill?	**Heeft u . . .?**
Have you got a menu?	
I'd like a telephone directory	**Ik zou graag . . .**
*I'd like some sandwiches	
*Where can I get some newspapers?	**Waar kan ik . . . krijgen?**
Where can I get a cup of tea?	
Is there a key?	**Is er een sleutel?**
Is there a timetable?	**Is er . . .?**
Is there a telephone directory?	
Is there a menu?	

*Are there any keys?	**Zijn er sleutels?**
*Are there any newspapers?	**Zijn er . . . ?**
*Are there any sandwiches?	

Now make up more sentences along the same lines. Then try these new phrases:

Ik wil graag . . . (I'll have . . .)
Ik heb . . . nodig (I need . . .)

I'll have a glass of beer	**Ik wil graag een glas bier**
I'll have a cup of tea	**Ik wil graag . . .**
I'll have some apples	
I need a cup of tea	**Ik heb een kop thee nodig**
I need a key	**Ik heb . . . nodig**
*I need some newspapers	**Ik heb kranten nodig**
*I need some keys	
*I need some addresses	
*I need some sandwiches	
*I need some suitcases	

SOME/ANY

In cases where *some* or *any* refer to more than one thing, such as *some/any newspapers* and *some/any tomatoes,* there is no Dutch equivalent, as explained earlier.

(some/any) newspapers	**kranten**
(some/any) tomatoes	**tomaten**

As a guide, you can usually *count* the number of containers or whole items. In cases where *some* refers to a part of a whole thing or an indefinite quantity, the word **wat** can be used.

Look at the list below and complete the missing items

the butter	de boter	wat boter	some butter
the bread	het brood	wat brood	some bread
the cheese	de kaas	wat kaas	some cheese
the coffee	de koffie	wat koffie	some coffee
the ice-cream	het ijs	...	some ice-cream
the lemonade	de limonade	...	some lemonade
the pineapple	de ananas	...	some pineapple
the sugar	de suiker	...	some sugar
the tea	de thee	...	some tea
the water	het water	...	some water
the wine	de wijn	...	some wine

Practise saying and writing these sentences in Dutch:

Have you got some ice-cream?	Heeft u wat ijs?
Have you got some pineapple?	
I'd like some butter	Ik zou graag wat boter hebben
I'd like some sugar	
I'd like some bread	
Where can I get some cheese?	Waar kan ik wat kaas krijgen?
Where can I get some ice-cream?	
Where can I get some water?	
Is there any water?	Is er wat water?
Is there any lemonade?	
Is there any wine?	
I'll have some beer	Ik wil graag wat bier
I'll have some tea	
I'll have some coffee	

THIS AND THAT

There are two words you can use when pointing:
dit (this), dat (that)
If you don't know the Dutch name for an object, just point and say:

Ik zou graag dat hebben	I'd like that
Ik wil graag dit hebben	I'll have this
Ik heb dat nodig	I need that

HELPING OTHERS

You can help yourself with phrases such as:

I'd like . . . a sandwich	Ik zou graag . . . een dubbele boterham
Where can I get . . . a cup of tea?	Waar kan ik . . . een kop thee . . . krijgen
I'll have . . . a glass of beer	Ik wil graag . . . een glas bier
I need . . . a bill	Ik heb . . . een rekening . . . nodig

If you find a compatriot having trouble making himself/herself understood, you should be able to speak to the Dutch person on his/her behalf. A pronunciation guide is provided from here on.

He'd like . . .	**Hij zou graag een cake** hey zow hrahk en cake
She'd like . . .	**Zij zou graag een cake** zey zow hrahk en cake
Where can he get . . . ?	**Waar kan hij een kop thee krijgen?** war kun hey en kop tay krey-hen
Where can she get . . . ?	**Waar kan zij een kop thee krijgen?** war kun zey en kop tay krey-hen
He'll have . . .	**Hij wil graag een glas bier** hey wil hrahk en hlus beer
She'll have . . .	**Zij wil graag een glas bier** zey wil hrahk en hlus beer
He needs . . .	**Hij heeft zeep nodig** hey hayft zape nodik
She needs . . .	**Zij heeft zeep nodig** zey hayft zape nodik

You can also help a couple or a group if they are having difficulties. The Dutch word for *they* is zij.

They'd like . . .	**Zij willen graag een krant** zey willen hrahk en krunt
Where can they get . . . ?	**Waar kunnen zij een reisgids krijgen?** wahr koonen zey en reys-hits krey-hen
They'll have . . .	**Zij willen graag wat brood** zey willen hrahk wut brote
They need . . .	**Zij hebben wat wijn nodig** zey hebben wut weyn nodik

What about the two of you? No problem. The word for *we* is **wij**.

We'd like ...	**Wij willen graag wat wijn** *wey willen hrahk wut weyn*
Where can we get ...?	**Waar kunnen wij sleutels krijgen?** *wahr koonen wey slertels krey-hen*
We'll have ...	**Wij willen graag het menu** *wey willen hrahk et mer-noo*
We need ...	**Wij hebben de rekening nodig** *wey hebben der rayker-ning nodik*

Try writing out your own checklist for these four useful phrase-starters like this:

Ik zou graag ...	**Wij willen graag ...**
Hij zou graag ...	**Zij willen graag ...**
Zij zou graag ...	
Waar kan ik ... krijgen?	**Waar kunnen wij ... krijgen?**
Waar kan hij ... krijgen?	**Waar kunnen zij ... krijgen?**
Waar kan zij ... krijgen?	

MORE PRACTICE

Here are some useful Dutch names of things. See how many different sentences you can make up, using the various points of information given earlier in this section.

		singular	plural
1	ashtray	asbak (c)	asbakken
2	bag	tas (c)	tassen
3	car	auto (c)	auto's
4	cigarette	sigaret (c)	sigaretten
5	corkscrew	kurketrekker (c)	kurketrekkers
6	deckchair	ligstoel (c)	ligstoelen
7	garage (repairs)	garage (c)	garages
8	grapes	druif (c)	druiven
9	ice-cream	ijsje (n)	ijsjes
10	melon	meloen (c)	meloenen
11	passport	paspoort (n)	paspoorten
12	drying-up cloth	theedoek (c)	theedoeken
13	salad (lettuce)	krop sla (c)	kroppen sla
14	shoe	schoen (c)	schoenen
15	stamp	postzegel (c)	postzegels
16	station	station (n)	stations
17	sunglasses	zonnebril (c)	zonnebrillen
18	telephone	telefoon (c)	telefoons
19	ticket	kaartje (n)	kaartjes

Index

Notes